ENTREPRENEURSHIP
EMPOWERED

ENTREPRENEURSHIP
EMPOWERED

A New Millennium Business Guide
from Start Up to Succession

NATASHA M PALUMBO

Eternal Enterprise Publishing

First Printing: 2019

Second Edition Printing: 2020

ISBN: 978-1-7344905-1-0

Author Bio Photograph By: Juan Padilla with Luxus Photos

Book Cover Designed By: Joanne Jenkins and Natasha Palumbo with Ldy Bug Images

Edited By: Lauren Michelle

Eternal Enterprise Publishing
Sacramento, CA Ordering Information:

Special discounts are available on quantity purchases by corporations, associations, educators, and others. For details, contact the publisher at the above listed address.

U.S. trade bookstores and wholesalers:
Please contact Natasha M Palumbo
Tel: (916) 470-3330 or email natasha@entrepreneurshipempowered.com

Dedication

To my beautiful children, Allan and Annabella, I will love you for all time and eternity. You are my very reasons for living the EMPOWERED life. I encourage you to remember that love is the only thing that is real. Everything else is an illusion. Remember to always operate out of love, starting with yourselves, and be EMPOWERED!
You are both amazing!
You are Palumbos!

Contents

Acknowledgments

Father God, I thank You for the beautiful gift of life, Your eternal love, and amazing grace. Without You, I am nothing. But through You, I am Natasha M Palumbo, the daughter of the Most High. All honor and glory to Your name.

To my parents, I am eternally grateful. You all gave me several different gifts. Many of which you will see displayed in this book. Mom, thank you for the gift of creativity and a poetic use of words. Daddy and Bonnie, thank you for the gift of entrepreneurship. Remember there is no shame in speaking our truth, the good, the bad, and the ugly. In doing so we release ourselves from the bondage, take the keys back to our life, and become *Empowered!* I love you all.

To my best friend, Joanne Jenkins, thank you for being the one true person outside of my children that I trust with all of me. Thank you for all the support, not only for the time you have given to me during the writing of my book, but for all the constant support in my life. I am grateful for you. You are not only my best friend, you are my sister.

To my students, who inspired me to write *Entrepreneurship Empowered*, you are all very special to me. Professor P loves each of you and encourages you to live your life to the fullest. Dream and Do.

To my dear friend and mentor, Ron Hickey, thank you for guiding me through the writing process. For helping rewire my brain. For all the wisdom you bestowed upon me at each of our encounters. You are ridiculously amazing!

To my earthly angel who will remain unnamed, you completely saved me and blessed me a thousand-fold. I am eternally grateful, and I pray you receive a thousand back for all you have done for me. Thank you is simply not enough, but for now it will have to do.

Preface

To the reader, I want to thank you for your support. The fact that you are reading this book tells me that you are ready to be an Empowered Entrepreneur. You will find a wealth of information in this book. *Entrepreneurship Empowered* is full of up-to-date tools, strategies, and resources that will help you in life and business.

I am in the business of building up people who build businesses. I am honored to be able to help you build, too. You may visit my website at the address listed below. There you will find all the services and products I offer. I am a business adjunct professor with several colleges in the state of California, as well as a coach and consultant. I have been an entrepreneur since 2002. I am passionate about business and education. In addition to teaching, I host several workshops in the U.S., and I have a virtual *Entrepreneurship Empowered* online program. I firmly believe that we can and should live an *EMPOWERED* life. I would love for you to connect with me. You can find me on both LinkedIn and Instagram @ Natasha M Palumbo.

Be well,
Natasha M Palumbo, MBA

Author, Coach, Consultant, and Speaker
Entrepreneur – Educator – Empowered

www.entrepreneurshipempowered.com

Introduction: *Entrepreneurship Empowered*

"The man who understands how something is done will always be employed. The man who understands why something is done, will always be the boss of the man who only knows how. But the woman who owns the company and bends the arch of sexism understands the true and ultimate power of ambition."

—Ronald T. Hickey, author

I come from a deep history of poverty, abuse, and neglect. I have faced more in the first two decades of my life than most humans ever will. But I am a LION. Did you know that the world we live in is a jungle? There are all kinds of animals in this jungle, and you will need to familiarize yourself with all of them—especially if you desire to be successful in business. You will either eat or be eaten. It is up to you to decide which one you are going to do or be.

I am the first in my family to hold a master's degree, let alone be a woman in that category. I have been chosen in this life to be a generational curse breaker and a generational blessing maker. I have worked extremely hard and will always work hard for all that I desire. That is the key to business. Hard work pays off. Doing what you love is possible. Dreams can become a reality. Nothing is impossible.

In 1999, I began working for Start To Finish Files, a California-based legal and medical copy service that specializes in Social Security disability law. I was hired by Dan Acland, who founded the business in 1994. This man changed the entire direction of my life. Little did I know at that time that I would become the owner of Start To Finish Files. At that time, I was going to school to be a high school photography teacher. I have a K-12 education background, which serves me well today. Dan hired me on the spot. When I started at his company, I used to push around a gurney with a small copy machine on it. You should have seen me trying to get this big gurney around places. It was hilarious! And you can only imagine the looks I got. But it was a job, and it had a lot of flexibility, which worked perfectly for me while I attended school.

Dan hired me to work at the Sacramento and Stockton locations. He had four other locations in the Bay Area that he handled with another employee. In 2002, Dan came to me and told me he was going to sell the business. He was planning on returning to school to work on his PhD in economics. I, at the time, was a welfare mom. I didn't make much money working because it was only a part-time gig and I was going to school. I had no money to buy the business. I tried to look for resources to help me purchase it but to no avail.

But did you know that one moment can change a thousand after it? Well, here was that one moment for me. One Sunday morning, Dan called. I answered the phone, and I will never forget what he said: *"Natasha, I am going to sell you the business. I am selling it to you for $20,000, and I will give you $4,000 start-up cash—$2,000 one month, and $2,000 the next month. I have you set up for a two-year* *payment plan. I have a small interest that will be included, and I have calculated all of it. There is enough money being generated that you will be able to make payments, cover all costs for the business, and still make a profit. It is yours.*" I fell to the floor in tears. Let me say this one more time: I was a welfare mom. I had been on welfare for some time. Being on welfare is humiliating. You are often treated like the scum of the earth. But again, it only takes one moment to change a thousand after it.

On July 16, 2002, I became the new owner of Start To Finish Files (STFF), and it became my new legal name. I purchased the business with six locations in half the state of California, a small staff, some equipment, all the clients, and the name. Oh, that glorious name. Just like Ray Kroc, who joined McDonald's after the McDonald brothers had franchised it, I had to have that name. There is power in a name. I am everything of that name. You can be assured that whatever I start, I will finish.

I wasted no time in my pursuit to build and grow STFF. Within the first year of ownership, I expanded to Santa Barbara, California. Then, less than a year later, I expanded to Southern California with the help of my truest and most trusted employee, Joanne Jenkins. I picked up seven more locations. Business doubled, and we were booming. And just as planned, in 2004, I had fully paid off STFF and was debt-free. Imagine that. A welfare mom now a powerful CEO of her own company. Ambition!

My growth didn't stop there. I picked up more locations in Arizona and Nevada. By 2006, I was sitting at seventeen locations in three states. The work was flowing. I increased in all areas—from clients to staff to locations. It was amazing. I started to grow even more. For a number of months, work was coming in from the East Coast because there was a backlog of files that needed to be processed. California was chosen to do that work. So, Florida and Georgia were sending their work to my locations, and I was the copy service of choice, so, of course, the work came to me.

Now I had new clients, and when they started to receive the excellent customer service and reliability I gave them, they told me if I ever came to Florida or Georgia, they would make sure I had work. I said, *"Oh, is that right?"* Then, I did it. I took a big leap of faith and I expanded to the East Coast. I spent one full summer in 2007 building business in Florida and Georgia. My clients welcomed me with open arms and files galore. Work was everywhere. STFF had now grown into twenty-seven locations in five states.

"What you spend years building could be destroyed overnight; build anyways."

—Mother Teresa, missionary

That is my favorite quote by Mother Teresa. I always add that *"you never know what you are* left *with in the rubble. Perhaps a diamond in the rough, which is you."* I am that diamond, and I am that quote. After a great run, STFF slowly started declining. Can you guess why? Technology. I am a copy service. Ironically, the year I bought my business, the Social Security Administration started moving toward an electronic filing system. Paper records were going to be no more. Or, that is what we thought. There is still paper today, of course, but very little. It did take the Social Security Administration a full decade to move most of the records from paper to paperless, but nevertheless, it did take place, and it had a major impact on my thriving and growing business.

Just as Georgia and Florida starting booming, California started to decline. I had already known that paper would dissolve, even when growing my business to the East Coast. Several people questioned why I would even attempt to expand to the East Coast with the knowledge that the industry was dying. But let me ask you this question: At one point in our lives, we will give up the ghost; we will die.... Do we stop growing just because we have the knowledge of death? Absolutely not! There was money on the table, and they were telling me that it was mine for the taking. All I had to do was get up and go get it. See, it was that simple. Get up and go get what is rightfully yours. That is exactly what I did.

I had a very nice growth period while doing business in Georgia and Florida. One of the coolest parts of growing my business to the East Coast was that I had a location in my hometown of Fort Myers. That is where I was born and raised. I left there in 1996, and there I was, back home doing business—not only there, but in six other locations in Florida. I was very proud of all my hard work. Little did I realize that a flatline was coming. I mean, I knew my run wouldn't last forever, but I was certainly hoping I could last a little longer than I did. One day, it just hit. The files had dried up. Florida and Georgia were no more. Only California still had files. Nothing like before, but enough to keep me busy. I had no more employees. My equipment had changed from a copy machine to a scanner and a laptop. I was doing all I could to survive, and I was struggling emotionally. My baby, STFF, was dying.

STFF changed my entire life. It took me from welfare to wealth, and it was looking like I might be heading back to welfare. I continued to do all I could to stay in the game. I started scanning records, specifically closed records, and to this day, I still scan for one of my longest-standing clients, Patrick Kelly. I have been scanning his records for a very long time. He is my faithful client, and I am so grateful for him. Scanning, however, didn't last that long because the economy crashed. When it did, even those with money held on to the change they had. It was dark times for our country and our people. Secondly, scanners started becoming more accessible and more user-friendly. So, again, out went the middleman, and the internal staff was given the task to handle scanning.

In Social Security disability law, there are court reporters called "verbatim hearing monitors." They use a keyboard and a recording system to document the disability hearing. They are contract workers. Many of my clients recommended that I try to bid on one of the contracts, and that was exactly what I did. The first time I put in a bid on the contract, they closed it without hiring any contractors. Some funding issues came up. I continued to watch for it, and it opened again. By this time, I was attending California State University, pursuing my master's degree in business administration. I was almost done, and I thought of how great it would be to transition from graduate school into a new season with STFF.

I bid on a contract to be a verbatim hearing monitor and won sixteen federal contracts in the state of California. The contract was worth up to $1.5 million over a five-year period. Because my copy service was so well-known for superior customer service and reliability, it was an easy win. Shortly after, I graduated with my master's and gave birth to my daughter. I started working as a clerk, predominately in Sacramento, San Rafael, and San Francisco, and held open contracts in other locations.

Clerking was interesting but short-lived. In Sacramento, I had a judge who thought I was too big to be in his presence. I have struggled with my weight most of my life due to the intense amount of trauma I have endured. I had just given birth to my daughter and had gone through one of the most painful events of my life. I pretty much lost my business, my home that I lived in for almost a decade, and damn near my mind. I was carrying a lot of weight— physically, mentally, and emotionally. But it was the physical weight you could see, and he didn't like that I was a heavy-set woman.

The Social Security Administration tried to take away all my locations, but my judges in other offices came to my rescue and spoke on behalf of my work ethic and character. I was able to keep everything but Sacramento. This, however, made it increasingly hard for me to work, as I now had to travel several hours to earn money. But I did what I needed to do. I clerked for almost two years. Then, the Social Security Administration decided they were going to pause the contracts and have in-house staff do the clerking. It was a big mess and it didn't last very long, but by that point, I had moved on.

While I was clerking, I learned more and more about Social Security disability law. My judges encouraged me to practice law. In Social Security disability law, you can practice as an attorney or as a non-attorney. As a non-attorney, you can be paid just as much as an attorney if you pass the test given by the federal government. I had both attorneys and non-attorneys as my clients, so I was aware that there were two different types, but I didn't know much more than that. I told some of my closest clients that I was considering working as a non-attorney. They were all very supportive. I began to study the Code of Federal Regulations—parts 400 to 499. I paid to take the test and flew myself to Baltimore. I passed. I had now become my own client and spin-off of STFF. And STFF Disability Advocacy Group was born.

I did some work for another non-attorney and I won the case, but she felt like I didn't deserve to receive the monetary split, which was $6,000. At that point, I was done. I wanted nothing more to do with Social Security disability law. I decided not to practice, and I turned my attention to pursuing teaching. One of the main reasons I earned my master's degree was to teach at the college level. I had always wanted to be a teacher. As I said earlier, prior to buying and taking ownership of my business, I was going to school to be a high school photography teacher. I had been a guest teacher and speaker ever since I graduated with my bachelor's degree.

I was shifting so fast at this point, and I was struggling financially. I had to stabilize my financial health. I still had STFF, but there was very little work—certainly not enough to live off of. The contracts were gone, and I was not practicing. I started applying for state jobs and was hired by the State of California Department of Transportation. It was the worst eighteen months of my life. I was never built to be a nine-to-five worker. I am a workhorse who will work around the clock—I am an Empowered Entrepreneur, damn it. During the same time that I applied for state jobs, I also applied for the faculty diversity internship with Los Rios Community College District. I had found out about the program a year prior but missed the application deadline by three days. When it opened again, I was ready. My application was accepted, and I was selected for an interview. Mind you, I'm a pretty polished educator, but at that time, I was nervous. In the teaching demo, I failed to state my name. One could see my nerves, I'm sure. I can still remember walking out of my new state job office with my cell phone in my hand, reading the email from Los Rios telling me that I was not selected for the internship. I was crushed. I called my son and just cried. He said, *"Mom, one blessing at a time. You just got the state job; it is not time for the internship. It doesn't mean it won't happen. It just means it wasn't going to happen this year."*

Oh, the wisdom of our youth. He was right. One blessing at a time. I was able to stabilize by working the state job, and my financial health recovered. Then, a year passed, and the faculty diversity internship opened again. You already know what I did. I applied! The application and all supporting documents were ready to go. I was selected for an interview, and trust and believe me, I was not going to forget my name this time. I went into the interview with full confidence. I knocked the teaching demo out of the park. I remember telling Dolly, my interviewer, that I had been waiting for this moment for three years. I explained how I found out about the internship three years prior, but the application had closed three days prior to finding out. Then I explained that the next year I was selected for an interview but forgot to say my name. She said, *"You have waited three years for this?"* *"Yes, ma'am,"* I replied, *"and hopefully the wait is now over."*

It was just a little over three weeks later that the congratulatory email came in. I was elated. I mean, beaming with joy and bursting at my seams with excitement! One moment changes a thousand after it. You remember me telling you that, right? This was that one moment, yet again.

I started the internship in the fall of 2014. We had eight weeks of coursework. We met once every Saturday. Then, in the spring of 2015, we were able to co-teach.

Now I told you I hated the state job, so I left it. I left in about the second week of November 2014. I was just starting my internship with Los Rios and I already knew that being a professor is what I would be doing, and no matter what, I would be fine. God was with me. He had never failed me, and He would not now. Leap of faith once again. (You will see this is a theme for me.)

There I was, no longer surviving but rather thriving. I was glowing on a daily basis. The internship validated that, indeed, being a college professor was one of the callings in my life. The coolest part about the internship was that I was able to co-teach at Sacramento City College. That was the college I attended and where I earned my associate's degree in photography. I had come full circle. I was giving back, which I love to do. I have used education as the foundation of a better life, and today it serves as the scaffold to building the life I have always dreamed of having. Sacramento City College was where my metamorphosis began in 1998. Now I was back, and I was reaching the student body I once was a part of. It was empowering, to say the least.

After the internship, I hit the ground running. I was grinding and grinding in pursuit of a teaching job. Finally, in the spring of 2016, I was hired at Sierra College. I was hired to teach one class in the fall of 2016—Business 20: Introduction to Business. Right before the fall of 2016 began, my department chair reached out and told me she had not just one more class, but two additional classes for me to teach. One more Business 20, and Business 140: Small Business Management and Entrepreneurship.

I was floored. It was all I could do to contain myself. I had been told NO for so long and so many times that—truth be told—I was slowly losing heart. But I am gritty. I never give up on my goals and dreams. I understood a very powerful principle that I will share with you now:

"You have RIGHTS to your NO, and your YES is UNDENIABLE!"

—Natasha M Palumbo, author and educator

I need all of you to understand this valuable Palumbo Principle. Your YES is far more powerful and purposeful than any NO you will ever receive. My YES is seven figures, eight when I leave this earth. My YES is speaking to seas upon seas of people in many nations. My YES is 6'4" and fine, and when he finally arrives, he will be right on time. The dice of life will throw you a NO time and time again. I want you to pick those dice up, shake them in your hand, spit on them if you need to, and throw them back to the world and, with everything you have inside you, say, "MY YES IS UNDENIABLE!"

Today, I not only work at one community college, but four—and one state university. I inspire classrooms full of students, and when they leave me, they leave *EMPOWERED* with the keys to their life. I have given them the gift of their authentic selves, which is the greatest gift of all. Being an Empowered Entrepreneur is just a bonus. They get that, too, but it's nothing compared to the gift of self with no shame, freedom to live in their rightful place in the world, and, most importantly, to be matrix-free.

I have shared with you the core of my entrepreneurial journey to date, but I didn't tell you everything. I am a serial entrepreneur. I have owned other businesses, and I am still building new ones to this day. I have had a photography business for a little longer than I have had STFF, but it has been more of a love than a business. I have made a nice sum of money doing it, and I still work on it today. I love it more than anything, and if you know any artist, they are normally starving, but I was much wiser. I have used it as a residual income source, and today it remains. I first started the business as Ldy Bug Images. Today, I use my name: Natasha Palumbo Professional Photography. Most of my work comes via word of mouth. I promise you that word of mouth is your best marketing tool around. It is how I grew STFF, as well as my photography business.

In 2005, I purchased a tanning salon because, well, I just simply didn't already have enough to do. My salon was called Italian Tans. It had a short run of just slightly over a year. I did very well in the business and had just over 300 clients come through my doors, but it was connected to a gym that was a money pit, and I could no longer do it. I had to close the doors. I sold all my beds, furniture, and mirrors. I had one stand-up bed that I had bought for $300.00.... I flipped it for $3,000. You can do the math on that one. That was lovely. I made really good money on liquidating all the equipment and the like. Then, I moved forward and focused my attention on STFF and Ldy Bug Images.

Due to all the experience I had, which now is expertise, I launched a consulting firm in 2010 and started working with small business owners one-on-one. I help analyze and correct organizational matters, review financial records in the pursuit of cash flow efficiencies and increased financial health, design and deliver trainings, and create systems and set them in place. I work with top management and provide them with my time and talents as they are needed. I have saved my clients hundreds of thousands of dollars, which they were able to return to their business and use for future growth. I have been instrumental in saving many small businesses that were failing due to their owner's lack of knowledge and skills. I still work as a business consultant and meet with clients on a regular basis. From start-up to succession, I work with them at all levels.

Finally, I have been serving the homeless since 2004. My organization is called the STEEL Legacy, which stands for *Serve, Teach, Encourage, Empower, and Lead.* This is my heart. I told you earlier, I love to give back. I will always extend my time and talents to those whom society has deemed unimportant. I have an outreach once every quarter. The fall outreach is normally held between October and November. It is dedicated to providing a full meal, along with other items, such as socks or rain gear. The winter outreach is held between December and January. It is dedicated to keeping the homeless warm. Did you know the homeless actually freeze to death? Yet, churches go empty Monday through Saturday. (I'll leave that one alone, though.) The spring outreach is held between March and April. It is dedicated to hygiene. The summer outreach is dedicated to keeping cool, sunblock, and water. All the water we can get. Cold water. Just as the homeless die from the cold, they also die from the heat.

At every outreach, we provide some type of food. We also provide small first aid kits. My thought is, if I can help them with a small wound they have on their body, they may not get so sick inside. We also make sure to provide water in every outreach. I wish I could say that each year we serve fewer and fewer people who are homeless, but that is not the case. We increase. Homelessness is an epidemic directly tied to mental health. It will require intense work to be fully cured—if ever.

Now you have been introduced to Start To Finish Files (STFF), Ldy Bug Images, Italian Tans, and the STEEL Legacy, but more importantly, to Natasha M Palumbo, the LION who runs the jungle. Today, I am in the business of building up people who build businesses. I call them my students and clients. I deliver to them the keys of freedom, equipping them with the tools, resources, and even possible opportunities for funding to make their business dreams come true.

My journey in academia has been interesting, to say the least. What I have found is that the books are subpar, and many textbooks are overpriced. I finally found my students a free online book, which I somewhat like, but it is dated. My goal from the moment I started my journey in pursuit of becoming a professor was to always be able to bring my students, and really any audience I could get my hands on, the most current, up-to-date information available. I will always share the truth of business. Not what the textbooks want to tell you, but rather what my life experience has been. What I know works—what real Empowered

Entrepreneurs are doing, and what real investors are looking for.

As you have seen thus far, I have been a very successful businesswoman. I bent the arch of sexism, and I owned the company. I have ambition, and I believe you do, too. I am Professor Palumbo, your new millennium professor. I am here to help you be matrix-free. Are you ready? If so, I can guarantee you that this book is an essential tool that will help you not only be matrix-free, but it will help you in business and in life.

This book is broken down into ten different interactive chapters and is very much a hands-on book. Several chapters will feature call-to-action activities. I would encourage you to take time to do them as you work through this course. They are designed to incite you from within.

Chapter One will dive deeply into the core—which is you. It all starts with you. You are the business. Far too often, we adopt self-imposed limitations and keep our own selves in bondage. We will begin by exploring who you are, how you see yourself, and what your purpose is. You will be taught the importance of your "WHY," and you will create your "WHY" statement. Then we will go into what it takes to be an Empowered Entrepreneur, and you will find out if you have it or if you don't. I will reveal what it really takes, including the skills you must have, and, more importantly, the mindset. We will cover the following topics:

- Growth mindset
- Creative mind
- Visionary
- Emotional intelligence
- Grit

Chapter Two will cover communication and technology. In order to truly be an Empowered Entrepreneur, you must learn to be a master of communication. You will need to understand you are solving problems with your words. In everything you do in business, you will be communicating in some form. I have a love/hate relationship with technology. I believe most people do. We need it—this is true, as it has helped make business so much easier and more efficient—but far too often, it has made us lazy. Many machines and technologies today are doing things that man once did. I am confident that we will always need the human. The human has unique core characteristics that machines will never have. We are in the human economy—the most powerful economy ever—but we must learn how to work with machines and technologies because they are here to stay. We will cover the following topics:

- Four main types of communication
- Hardware and software
- Website and social media

Chapters Three through Six are dedicated to the planning process for *Entrepreneurship Empowered*. We will cover the following topics:

- Forms of ownership
- Business plans (all of them)
- Marketing plan
- Financial plan

What I will let you know right now is that Empowered Entrepreneurs do more than they plan. I had tremendous growth and then even more transformation, but what I had above all was execution. I am a master at execution.

"Innovation is rewarded. Execution is worshipped."

—Dr. Eric Thomas, motivational speaker

Chapter Seven is one that is near and dear to my heart because it is where you will find leadership. Leaders build up more leaders. I pride myself on being a great leader. A boss will tell you what to do, but a leader will show you. A leader will get on the ground with you. Truly great leaders are humble in many ways. This doesn't mean they are pushovers—trust that. They simply understand that there is no difference in their power if they are on the ground or standing on a chair, screaming and waving their hands around like a crazy person. They just look more insane on the chair than they do on the floor, in a place of humility. We will cover the following topics:

- Leadership
- Business ethics

Chapter Eight will broaden our understanding of human resources—how powerful the human capital is, the importance of taking good care of it, and how to ensure you are meeting all the requirements related to employees. We will cover the following topics:

- Human relations
- 21st century skills
- Gig economy

Chapter Nine will round us almost out the door. Most of the book is dedicated to planning, but here the tide shifts. We will move into what it looks like to officially launch your business, how to successfully manage your business, and, of course, how to grow your business. Many resources will be given in this chapter, and you will want to ensure that you explore those that best suit you and your business needs. We will cover the following topics:

- Launching your business
  - o Choose a business structure
  - o Choose your business name
  - o Register your business
  - o Get federal and state tax ID numbers
  - o Apply for licenses and permits
  - o Open business bank account
  - o Get business insurance
- Managing your business
  - o Manage your finances
  - o Hire and manage employees
  - o Pay taxes
  - o Stay legally compliant
  - o Close or sell your business

- Growing your business
  - Get more funding
  - Expand to new locations
  - Become a federal contractor

Chapter Ten will close us out, and I will share with you the 10 Core Palumbo Principles. I will leave you with what I feel is the most critical element in taking you from good to great, from great to amazing, and from amazing to ridiculously amazing. I live the principles and I believe deeply in them. It is my honor to share not only them, but this entire book of knowledge, wisdom, and insight, so that you may be *EMPOWERED* to live your best life as an Empowered Entrepreneur. The 10 Core Palumbo Principles are:

- Pay Yourself First
- Emotional Intelligence Is Key
- Stay Gritty
- Execution Is Required at All Times
- We Don't Predict Our Future; We Create It
- Sacrifice to Succeed
- The Four Agreements
- The Story of the Star
- You Have Rights to Your NO, and Your YES Is Undeniable
- The Way Out Is Within

My ambition bent the arch of sexism. Imagine that. A welfare mom who became a powerful CEO of her own company, then a professor who today stands before hundreds of students a semester and reaches them unlike any professor before. I am growing in the gift of speaking, and I am your next top female speaker in the world. I suffered from dyslexia and had trouble with comprehension, but you are now reading my book. One of several I will write. According to my very good friend and mentor, Ron Hickey, *"Your ambitions establish your limits more than any other aspect of your life. With ambition, you can overcome undereducation. With ambition, you can conquer underachievement. With ambition, you can become the next great CEO, author, doctor, politician, talk show host, national news anchor, and everything else you want to be— if you're up for the challenge."*

I promise you, many times I look insane on all levels of my mansion. But I have the Willy Wonka of all elevators. Would you like to get in? We are going to break through the ceiling, and you will be amazed at the view as we float around in the sky. Welcome to *Entrepreneurship Empowered!*

ENTREPRENEURSHIP EMPOWERED

 **Chapter 1**: The Mind of an *Empowered Entrepreneur*

"It takes courage to endure the sharp pains of self-discovery rather than choose to take the dull pain of unconsciousness that would last the rest of our lives."

—Marianne Williamson, author

Do you have what it takes? Being an Empowered Entrepreneur is not for the faint of heart. It requires intense discipline, sacrifice, wisdom, ability to handle setbacks with rigor, and very high emotional intelligence (EI). Talent will only take you so far, and knowledge must accompany you at every dance you attend. However, your ability to handle the ups and downs of the journey and become an Empowered Entrepreneur will require you to understand yourself above anything else. You will need to understand agreements that you have that are truly yours, and those that are programmed in you. Yes, every human being is programmed. I need you to find out your programming, and if you truly agree with all that your programming indicates you are. You must also address the elephant in the room: your trauma. Everyone in the world has trauma. Primary, secondary, or both. Just like no one gets out alive, no one gets away trauma-free. I am a trauma expert—not because of some fancy degree, but because I endured decades upon decades of trauma and have done intense work to heal, and more so, to be free of the torture of trauma. The torture of wounded emotion.

Logic will never win over wounded emotion. You must become emotionally intelligent. Then, and only then, will your logic win. Emotional intelligence allows you the space you need to hold emotion for yourself and then move forward in the facts of the case. You can have a deeper understanding of others by having high emotional intelligence. As we explore deeper, you will find that emotional intelligence is critical in leadership, management, dealing with clients, customer service, human relations, marketing, and so many other aspects of business. You must have emotional intelligence to be an Empowered Entrepreneur.

There are no set characteristics of an Empowered Entrepreneur. Sure, we are risk takers—you have probably heard that to be the most common trait. However, we are not extreme risk takers. We are not gamblers. Studies show that gamblers make very poor entrepreneurs, as they put too much on the table. On the contrary, we are calculated, strategic risk takers. I took a big risk by expanding my business to the East Coast. But I was very calculated and strategic in my pursuit of growth, just as I was when growing within California. Empowered Entrepreneurs do have one thing in common, however. Can you guess what it is?

"Whatever the mind can conceive and believe, the mind can achieve."

—Napoleon Hill, *Think and Grow Rich*

The mind is the common thread that connects all Empowered Entrepreneurs. There are two types of mindsets: fixed and growth. The fixed mindset is very constraining and keeps us bound. The growth mindset, on the other hand, is very liberating. The fixed mindset believes that talent and intelligence are all that's needed to be successful. The fixed mindset doesn't take well to criticism or failure, and normally only sees one way. The growth mindset believes that talent and intelligence, combined with hard work, will win every time. Even in failure, the growth mindset sees a winning score. The growth mindset is a lifelong learner and never turns down an opportunity to better oneself. The growth mindset understands the importance of practice and being dedicated to pursuing goals. The growth mindset goes through setbacks with an innate ability to persevere. The growth mindset is gritty.

The Empowered Entrepreneur has a growth mindset—also known as the entrepreneurial mindset. The entrepreneurial mindset sees opportunity where others see obstacles. It sees solutions where others only see fires. The entrepreneurial mindset has vision, and no vision is too radical, too far-fetched, or too insane. It believes that anything is possible; that no matter how long it takes, every dream will come to pass. The life desired is going to be lived. Nothing stops the entrepreneurial mindset. It is *EMPOWERED!*

How we see ourselves is directly related to how we will lead our lives. If you believe that your talents are fixed in stone, then you will stay stuck. You will keep repeating one hell of a rollercoaster ride by trying to prove yourself over and over again. You will stay in the valley of validation when you simply need to walk in the victory of being your authentic self. Stop wasting time trying to prove how great you are—try to grow and get better. When I work with business owners, I want to see them go from good to great, from great to amazing, and even then, I encourage them to keep growing. I want to see them struggle and go through growing pains. I encourage them to stretch themselves, to go to the ultra-limits of their lives. That is where they become ridiculously amazing. That is how you succeed in *Entrepreneurship Empowered.*

"The passion for stretching yourself and sticking to it, even (or especially) when it's not going well, is the hallmark of the growth mindset. This is the mindset that allows people to thrive during some of the most challenging times in their lives."

—Carol Dweck, Stanford psychologist

I would like you to take a moment to reflect on your mind and how you think. I know for some of you that could be a scary process. I can personally attest to having a very intense mind at times. I have battled in my mind. Many people do. You are not alone. I can directly relate it to my trauma. Side effects of abuse are nothing nice, and the battle of the mind is one of the most common side effects out there. But the mind is not a scary place. It is not fixed; it doesn't have to be, at least. The mind is wired intensely from our youth. That is where a great amount of our programming comes from. You can, however, rewire your mind. It takes time and it takes work, but it is worth it. For now, I would like you to discover what type of mindset you have.

There is a textbook that I use from time to time called *Entrepreneurship: The Practice and Mindset*, by Heidi M. Neck, Christopher P. Neck, and Emma L. Murray. The following mindset activity is derived from that book.[1] What does your mindset really say about you? I would like you to go to a place you haven't been to before. It can be a park, a restaurant, a library, really just about anywhere. It just needs to be unfamiliar. Take this book and a pen with you. I have provided space for you to write. For about five to ten minutes, I want you to look around. Gather your thoughts about what you see. You are now going to write your observations. You will use adjectives to describe what you see. For example, you may see a play structure at the park, but you need to describe it in detail. It may be shiny, empty, curved, broken, rusty, et cetera. You may then see a squirrel in the park. Is it cute, furry, ugly, mean, friendly? After you finish, I want you to sit down and look at the list of words you have before you. Circle all the words that have a positive connotation. Then I want you to put a square around all the words that have a negative connotation.

What is the point of all this, you may ask? The way we see the outside is a direct connection to our mindset. If you see the world as predominantly negative, then your mindset for *Entrepreneurship Empowered* needs to be further developed. If you have a more positive mindset, you will be able to see opportunities and make a difference.

What does your mindset say about you? Are you pleased with your mindset? Do you need to work on some areas? Do you struggle with seeing opportunities? I would like to encourage you that it is possible to change your mindset—doing so will change your life. I was, at one point in my life, living in a survival mindset. Poverty is a mindset. Being broke is just an illusion. Your rightful place is that you are an heir to the kingdom. But it is up to you to believe it within. You must stop walking in the forest of falsehood. You must realize you are the guard at the door of the kingdom. Only you are preventing yourself from walking through the door to claim your throne. *The way out is within.* Are you ready to be free? If you are free, would you like to grow even more? Keep reading.

Did you know that caterpillars have something called "imaginal cells"? They are cells that are, well, imagined. You see, once the caterpillar has eaten enough food, the new imaginal cells come forward. A new way of thinking begins. This becomes even more apparent after the struggle in the cocoon—the struggle for the caterpillar to morph into the beautiful butterfly it was purposed to be. The caterpillar and the butterfly both have a purpose, as each of us does. No matter what stage we are at in our lives, understanding our purpose is critical to being an Empowered Entrepreneur. You may not be purposed to be an entrepreneur, and this is perfectly okay. You have, however, been purposed to be *EMPOWERED!* You may be purposed to be a nurse and save lives. Or a comedian and keep us healthy by providing laughter, which is the best medicine. You may be a teacher who *EMPOWERS* your students. You may indeed be an entrepreneur. Each of us has natural talents and abilities which are given to us by the Creator. That Creator may look different to you than He does to me, but nevertheless, we were created, and through that creation we have more than just genetics in our DNA. We have our purpose and our calling. One of the things I love to ask my students and clients is, *"What did you play when you were little?"* The reason I ask this question is because that, my dear friends, is where the purpose is often held captive. I loved to play teacher when I was a little girl, and today I am just that: a teacher.

I am also an Empowered Entrepreneur and a caterpillar with imaginary cells—always excited for the transformation, even when I know it means a struggle will be accompanying it. Once you discover your purpose and your God-given talents, you will never be happy unless you are fully using them—not only in your life, but in your career as well. You will feel a void, and you will do many other things to fill that void but to no avail. I need you to move past any fear you have that the matrix has placed on you, and I need you to walk in your calling. Walk in your talents and authentic self. I can only attest from my own life that your gift will make room for you and you will never go without. When you combine the growth mindset with your God-given talents and abilities, you will be unstoppable. You will live like others only dream. You will leave a legacy worth ten generations or more. This is succession.

"You make your mark by being true to who you are and letting that be your staple."

—Kat Graham, actress

Your legacy becomes your "why?" Your "why" drives you from the moment you find it until the moment you leave this earth. Your "why" may slightly change over the years, but more often, it does not. You end up acquiring other "whys" along the way due to your own life metamorphosis. But for right now, I want you to take a few moments to think about your "why." Your "why" is also known as your impact statement. What impact do you desire to have in this world?

Your "why" can never be money. It must be something deeper. Your "why," along with your God-given talents and abilities, will steer you in life and keep you on course. I am going to share one of mine with you, then I want you to think about YOUR "why." I have provided space for you to write it out.

"My 'why' is deeply rooted in my desire to help others heal and be free from the trauma they have gone through in their lives. One out of every four girls is abused, and one out of every five boys is abused. I was abused from ages 3–13, then at ages 13–16, I went through another form of abuse. At age 16, I was a freshman in high school, and I was living on my own. This is only a portion of the abuse I endured. One of my greatest callings in life is to be used to help heal others. I will not only write a book, but I will write multiple books. I will also be speaking on a national and international level. I have many gifts that I plan to use fully. I have learned over time that I have been honored to have to endure what I have and still make it out. Now I give back!"

Now it is your turn. Give it a try. If you need time to think about it, then do that—think. Go to your core. Find your purpose within, and then write out your "why." After you find it, put it up where you can see it. Let it lead you in the direction that you truly desire to go.

_____

_____

_____

_____

_____

_____

_____

_____

_____

_____

ENTREPRENEURSHIP EMPOWERED

"Timing, perseverance, and ten years of trying will eventually make you look like an overnight success."

—Biz Stone, co-founder of Twitter

Entrepreneurship Empowered is not about the short game, but rather the long game. You must understand what it really takes to be an Empowered Entrepreneur and the truth behind being a business owner. It is hard, very hard. Some days, you will question your own sanity. You will need to be your best cheerleader and your toughest coach. You will work many years and possibly make no money at all. You will work long hours, weekends, holidays, and you will work when you are sick. In the infancy stage of being an entrepreneur, you will be unhealthy in many ways. You will skip meals, lose sleep, and have no social life whatsoever. You will be desperate for balance and truly need it, but your business will need you more. You could easily compare your business to a real human baby: it will keep you up in the middle of the night because it is hungry, it will require your attention, and, if you don't care for it, it will die. In the United States, parents often leave their newborn and young children in the hands of others so they can go live in the cube farm Monday through Friday, 8:00 a.m. to 5:00 p.m., just to provide for their children. But if a business is left in the care of someone other than the owner, it can be destroyed or stolen right out of the owner's hands. You must be on the ship and in control at all times. That is no easy task.

You are responsible for everything. Until your business gets up and running, you will need to be dressed up one moment to meet with potential clients, then, in the same day, you'll need to change your clothes to something you can clean in because the toilets need your attention—it's dirty and there is only you. You will grow if you are healthy because healthy things grow, and growing things change. In growth, you will be able to hire more people, and then your responsibilities grow even more. You are then responsible for your employees and their families. That is a BIG responsibility. They will be of great help to you if you are wise and able to hire solid, skilled employees, which there is a great shortage of in this world. A word of caution: hiring family and/or friends is not wise. It can backfire on you and you can lose longtime friendships, and family ties can be broken.

Failure is a reality. According to the Small Business Administration (SBA), nearly 50% of new businesses fail within the first five years.[2] You need to be able to handle the fact that your business may fail. That doesn't mean you will always fail or that one day you will not have a successful business, because you certainly can. Failure is just as important as success. Failure is what made Walt Disney great. His very first business went bankrupt. Failure creates change and forces us to learn. To be an Empowered Entrepreneur, you must constantly be learning. You are your number one investment, so you must deposit into your investment on a regular basis. Knowledge will give you the greatest return. Read books, go to conferences, meet on a regular schedule with a mentor or coach, take classes, travel to places you have never been to before. Decide now that you will be a lifelong learner. Even if you decide that entrepreneurship is not for you, you will still be a very wise human, and, more importantly, you will be awake. You will be *EMPOWERED!*

"Live the Life of Your Dreams: Be brave enough to live the life of your dreams according to your vision and purpose instead of the expectations and opinions of others."

—Roy T. Bennett, *The Light in the Heart*

Vision, just like purpose, is critical to *Entrepreneurship Empowered.* You may be surprised at how many major deals close on one fact: the investor can see that the Empowered Entrepreneur is a visionary. When you are a visionary, you bring the extraordinary to life. Your mindset is creative and not limited. Thought that is no longer limited will result in experiences that are no longer limited. The visionary knows this because their thoughts are not limited.

Visionaries are able to manifest. Vision boards are a great way to manifest your vision. I have several vision boards. I have seen many things come to fruition through my boards. When I create them, I not only think about the vision, but I have learned how to feel the vision bringing the heart and the mind together. If you are believing in rain for the desert, you must not just pray for it, you must feel the rain. You must smell the rain. You must be wearing rain gear and be prepared for the rain. This is the heart of vision—the feeling of it. If you truly want to succeed as an Empowered Entrepreneur, then you need to not only see yourself and your business succeeding, you need to feel it. You need to feel what it is like to wear imported silk suits. You need to feel what it is like to sit at the top of your high-rise office building. The feeling is the part that brings it to life.

Empowered Entrepreneurs do not predict the future; they create it. Your final task in this chapter will be to create a vision board.

There are several ways you can create your vision board. You can gather magazines and cut out pictures and words. You will need glue sticks and a poster board to place the pictures on. You can also use a computer and google different things that represent your vision and then save the pictures. Then take those pictures and place them in a Word document. You could even create it in Adobe Photoshop. You could use your smartphone (same concept as with a computer). Google the things you desire for yourself, business, life, family, and so on, then save the pictures to your camera roll. You will need a collage maker—there are many free apps out there that can make picture collages. Then place whichever pictures you like in the collage. TA-DA! You now have your vision board.

While creating the vision board, you really want to be connected in thought and heart. See yourself in the boat that you just cut out. Feel the breeze as you walk the beach and watch the sunset in the picture of Bali that is now on your board. See the increase in financial freedom and see that you are rich in love, time, talents, and the like. I use a lot of words in my vision boards, as words are my love language. What is your love language? If it is words, then make sure to use lots of positive words on your board.

The vision board needs to be placed where you can see it every day. If you created one on your phone, you may save it as your lock screen or background. You could even send it to be printed as a photograph. For your Word document boards, print them out in color if you can, but black and white will do. The poster board method is simple: just put that sucker up on your wall. Put them all up on your wall. Look at them. Let them breathe and live within you. Go back to feeling your vision and believing in it. Before you know it, you will be driving the Camaro you put on your board. You will be floating in a hot air balloon ride. You will be walking the streets of Rome. All of what I just listed, from the Camaro to Rome, were on my vision board and have come to reality. I could go on and on, but now I want you to give it a try.

Please remember this one thing: the vision is for an appointed time. Though it may tarry, it will not be late. For everything there is a season. You must be patient and just know that your vision will come to pass if you faint not.

Remember the caterpillar and the imaginal cells I told you about at the beginning of the chapter? They are its higher purpose cells. We, too, have such cells. They come forward as we transform our lives. Your vision is your imaginal cells. It is your higher purpose. I am sure the caterpillar had its doubts, and I can only imagine its friends and family gave it a hard time. *You're back imagining things, aren't you? You really believe you have a higher purpose? You are so low to the ground that the only thing that has you beat is a snake. Come on now. You think you will really fly one day?* Have you ever been mocked by your friends or family for what you imagined? What you believed your higher power to be? I have, and it hurt. But with the same confidence of a caterpillar that walked so low to the ground, I believed that I had imaginal cells—my higher purpose cells. And at the right time, in the right season, I would go into a very dark place. I would let go of my family, friends, and foes. I would transform, and then I would struggle just a little more. Finally, I would break through the cocoon. The most beautiful imagined butterfly you ever saw in your life.

Now go create your imaginal cells. It is time for you to grow. Healthy things grow. Growing things change. Change is good. You have the power in your mind to be whatever you desire. But faith is dead without work. And so is vision. You must execute. The remaining chapters will provide you with the knowledge and the tools you need to help increase your ability to execute. Before you know it, you will be flying in the air with me.

"Float like a butterfly. Sting like a bee."

—Muhammad Ali, World Champion boxer

Muhammad Ali was one of the greatest boxers of all time. His success is directly related to his ability to think systematically, which created thought patterns and processes that attracted greatness to him. He was a very skilled and talented boxer and would out-practice anyone. As an Empowered Entrepreneur, you need to be skilled like Ali. You need to have his same work ethic. You need to understand the power of your unique frequency, which is your thought process. You need to settle for nothing less than greatness. You will need to understand your unique talents. There are four talents that are critical to being an Empowered Entrepreneur:

- Imagination
- Experimentation
- Insight
- Wisdom

When was the last time you played? I mean freely played, when your imagination just ran wild. Do you remember being a child and playing without a care in the world? There are so many benefits to playing—most importantly, the ability to heighten our imagination. When we can imagine with no self-censorship getting in the way, no pressure from the matrix telling us we are getting it wrong, we become so liberated. So much learning can be found no matter what form of play you encounter. Imagination is sparked. As an Empowered Entrepreneur, it is important you develop the talent of imagination. It opens the mind, and when the mind is open, there is no limit to what it can and will produce. Imagination also activates creativity.

I am always surprised at the number of people who believe they are not creative. Now, I understand that some people are not that crafty. I get that part, but when mothers especially tell me they are not that creative, I think to myself, *How is that? You created a human, for God's sake!* Imagination and creativity open a whole new level of thinking for you. It is that key that finds solutions to problems. But do you know what blocks creativity? FEAR. Yes, fear. **F**alse **E**vidence **A**ppearing **R**eal. Fear is an emotional roadblock. Before we even get started being creative, fear pops in with self-doubt and insecurity. Then we self-censor. The mind is so powerful, but when limited, it is very weak. You must turn the self-censor off and stop dancing with your complex issue. Pick up the brush of creativity and paint your future. The Empowered Entrepreneur doesn't predict his or her future; they imagine it. They create it.

The talent of experimentation is why scientists are so damn cool. They experiment all the time. Without experimentation, we would not have many of the inventions we have today, nor would we have the future. Thomas Edison is one of my favorite inventors of all time. Do you know how many times he failed while creating the light bulb? So many times! But it was through experiment that he finally arrived at the light bulb, and that sucker is everywhere today. You will be required in *Entrepreneurship Empowered* to get out of the building and or office and go experiment. Go try your product on the consumer. Go test your theory in the marketplace. Then you will know which next steps to take with your services or products. Everything in *Entrepreneurship Empowered* is about action and trying. When you experiment, you become open to learning about how new processes would work for your organization and ways to effectively cut costs in order to help manage cash flow. Again, there is no limit to what experimenting can do for you as you launch, manage, and grow your business.

One of the best places for you to do some experimenting is at a makerspace. A makerspace is a collaborative workspace. Co-working spaces can also be rented for start-up businesses. You will find all kinds of elements at a makerspace—from 3D printers to sewing machines. Everything from coding to the creation of art takes place in a makerspace. It is a hub for genius and creativity. You can use most of the equipment found there. You will need to learn how to use the equipment first, of course, but after that, you are good to go. If you are in my class at one of the colleges or in my virtual course, you will be introduced to our makerspace. There are makerspaces everywhere—all you have do is search online for them, and I am sure you will find one in your area. I encourage you to go explore and experiment.

A study at the University of Michigan revealed that empathy levels in our world have dropped dramatically— "*College kids today are about 40 percent lower in empathy than their counterparts of 20 or 30 years ago.*"[3] I am so shocked at how much we just don't care for humankind. The skill of insight is critical to life and business. The definition of insight, according to the dictionary, is "*the capacity to gain an accurate and deep intuitive understanding of a person or thing.*" In essence, insight is being empathic. Being able to relate and understand your clients' needs or your customers' needs is the golden key to maintaining their loyalty and business. Being able to put yourself in someone else's shoes will open your mind, enabling you to create better solutions for them. You may create products or services that fit their needs which were unmet prior to your solutions. This is only one of the reasons why insight is so important to have, not only as an Empowered Entrepreneur, but as a human being.

Some people who are what we call "empaths" believe they are cursed. But I am here to set the record straight: you are far from cursed. You are gifted, and we need your gift more today than ever before.

Wisdom is timeless. Many people are wise with age, and some never carry wisdom at all because they do not take time to reflect. As an Empowered Entrepreneur, I demand action. I am results-driven. But I never negate the power of reflection, and in *Entrepreneurship Empowered*, you must have both action and reflection in equal measure. It is in the reflection that we gain wisdom. How often do you reflect? From how your day was, to giving a presentation at work. When reflecting, it is important to have a pen and notepad available, or your computer if you like. Write it all out, from the good to the bad to the ugly. Even reflecting on the weather or season is critical. Take note of the time of day and your energy level—all very important pieces to your puzzle. To be successful in any area, you must exercise wisdom and plan carefully. If wisdom is to bring you prosperity, joy, admiration, and longevity of life, then you must be disciplined to reflect daily.

Do you have what it takes to be an Empowered Entrepreneur? It all starts in the mind. You must have a mind that is up to the challenge. You must have the talents mentioned above operating in your life on a daily basis. You must go to your core and walk in your authentic self. You must get in the dirt and never be afraid of hard work. Life is short, even on the longest day. I need you to roll with the punches, and when the opportunity presents itself, go for it. If the opportunity doesn't present itself, I need you to reflect

WHY? What didn't you do in your mind to create that opportunity? Become emotionally intelligent. Be gritty.

I also encourage you to take the following assessment and find out what animal you are. This world, as I have already told you, is a jungle. You will either eat or be eaten. It is up to you which one you will do or be.

As I stated in my introduction, it is important to know what your most dominant animal is, but more so to understand that you have four animals. My dear friend, Jesse Ross, is an author, speaker, and personal and professional development coach. He is also 4-Animal certified. The 4 Animals is the DISC personality assessment tool used to improve communication and self-awareness.[4] According to Jesse, there are four animals that run any workplace: a lion, a flamingo, a chameleon, and a turtle. What if you knew how each one operates, communicates, and works? What if you knew that your overbearing personality could be used as a strength? Or that the fact that you are indecisive means you are adaptable? This assessment gives you a rating for all four animal traits. It also shows you what your natural level is, and what your adaptable level is. This focus is incredibly beneficial for understanding self and improving self. More so, the assessments give you information on how best to work with other animal types that you will find in life. The assessment will take you less than fifteen minutes to complete, but it will unlock a lifetime of traits that will show you how to influence your team, your boss, and your significant other in a whole new way. Invest in your influence today! You may contact Jesse Ross at www.mrjesseross.com and use the code ProfessorP to access the assessment at a discounted rate. If you take my class at any of the colleges, or if you take my online course, you will be exposed to Jesse Ross and learn more about the four animals.

I am a firm believer in the 4 Animals assessment. For me, it has been instrumental in growing as a person, but more so as an Empowered Entrepreneur. *The way out is within*. Self-awareness is the key that unlocks the door to the way in.

I am asking again: Do you have what it takes to be an Empowered Entrepreneur? In the space provided, I want you to write your answer. After that, I want you to spend a little time thinking about your life goals. I want you to write out what life goals you have. The reason for this is that in order to achieve the life you desire, you are going to need to work for it. Your life goals will help direct you to the career you truly desire and need to have in order to live the life you dream of having.

I want you to remember that you must be committed. People don't normally move past their initial interests. If you are committed, you will do what it takes, but if you are only interested, you will do what is convenient. This is why many people do not move past their interests. They stay in a place of convenience. You, however, cannot do that to yourself, especially if you plan to live an *EMPOWERED* life. Remember*, the way out is within*.

_____

_____

_____

_____

_____

_____

_____

_____

_____

_____

_____

_____

_____

_____

_____

_____

_____

ENTREPRENEURSHIP EMPOWERED

Chapter 2: Communication and Technology

"Communication—the human connection—is the key to personal and career success."

—Paul J. Meyer, author and speaker

Communication is at the core of everything we do. We are constantly communicating, even when we are sleeping. In the jungle, the animals all speak different languages. This is why it is critical that you understand not only what type of animal you are, but also how to speak with the other animals in the jungle. A person who has the traits of a turtle is going to want all the details. They are going to want you to open up as much as you possibly can, and then they are going to want more. A lion, on the other hand, will get very pissed off if you give them too many details and do not get right to the point. They are only concerned with the point.

What the hell is the point?! In business and in life, you are going to need to master communication. I am currently building a speaking empire, and I work with one of the best in the business: Kendall Ficklin. He is my coach. I am a very proud member of Mr. Ficklin's organization, Grindation. You can learn more about him and Grindation at www.grindation.com.[5] If you have any interest in the business of speaking and coaching, I highly recommend his services. He is always dropping gems when he speaks to us, and he is constantly telling us how important it is to be an effective communicator and that everything revolves around our ability to communicate effectively. Many times, he shares with us conversations he has had with either clients or potential clients. We are able to listen and learn. I gain so much every time he shares.

Because communication is so important, I waste no time teaching it to my students—I place it at the top of each semester. It is also why I have placed it in this book as Chapter Two. In the new millennium, communication is rapidly changing and will continue to do so. However, we must understand some very solid principles of communication.

According to Merriam-Webster, **communication** is defined as "*a process by which information is exchanged between individuals through a common system of symbols, signs, or behavior.*" Business communication is used for a wide variety of activities including, but not limited to: strategic communications planning, media relations, public relations (which can include social media, broadcast and written communications, and more), brand management, reputation management, speech writing, customer-client relations, and internal employee communications.

There are different types of communication for this chapter. We will cover the top four: nonverbal, verbal, written, and visual. A business dictionary defines **nonverbal communication** as "*behavior and elements of speech aside from the words themselves that transmit meaning. Non-verbal communication includes pitch, speed, tone and volume of voice, gestures and facial expressions, body posture, stance, and proximity to the listener, eye movements and contact, and dress and appearance.*" We communicate nonverbally more often than we do verbally. Dr. Albert Mehrabian, author of *Silent Messages*, conducted several studies on nonverbal communication. He found that 7% of any message is conveyed through words, 38% through certain vocal elements, and 55% through nonverbal elements (facial expressions, gestures, posture, etc.).[6] Subtracting the 7% actual vocal content leaves one with 93%. Statistically speaking, 93% of communication is nonverbal. Can you believe that?

You need to understand that everything about you communicates—from the way you dress, to how you smell, to what comes out of your mouth, to how you listen. This is why it is important to take good care of yourself. I am always striving to become better than I was yesterday. Personal growth is very important to me, and I would encourage you to keep personal growth at the forefront of your mind. With regard to clothing, especially in business, you want to make sure you keep a professional look. This doesn't mean you need to wear a dress, a pantsuit, or a suit and tie all the time. It does, however, mean that you need to be presentable and have a clean appearance. You need to smell good. I can promise you this much, you don't have to be rich to dress well and smell good. Any thrift store in town has quality clothing at a discounted rate. You just need to go look. There are also several nonprofit organizations that offer professional clothing to those who are in need. And they offer it for free. I share this with you because I understand what it is like to not have a lot of money. But style and class I have always had, with or without money. As far as smell goes, a nice bath, brushing of the teeth, and deodorant should be enough. You don't want to wear too much perfume or cologne because the scent can be overpowering. A nice light scent should do the trick. When you look your best, you normally feel your best. This is another reason why you want to make sure you are always dressing to impress, even if it is just you that you are impressing.

Verbal communication is defined as *"the sharing of information between individuals by using speech. Individuals working within a business need to effectively use verbal communication that employs readily understood spoken words, as well as ensuring that the enunciation, stress and tone of voice with which the words are expressed is appropriate."* Communication, just as with many things in life, starts on the inside. Remember, *the way out is within.* You must be comfortable with yourself to effectively communicate with others. How do you communicate with yourself? What things are you saying to yourself?

Intrapersonal communication is also known as self-talk. Self-talk can be either positive or negative. For many years, I suffered with horrible self-talk. I would wander, far more than I care to admit, in the forest of falsehood and just sit under a tree of lies. Fatigued from my travels and all I carried, I would just sit and weep as the tree continually dropped lie after lie.

Then, I finally got up and became *EMPOWERED.* I took the keys to my life back, and I changed the way I communicated. First and foremost, with myself. Upon doing so, I worked on becoming a better communicator. I learned how to draw with my words. You will see me do it many times in this book. For me, communicating verbally means I need to show my story, not tell it. I need to bring it to life. It also means that I need to be authentic and real with those I am communicating with. In business, we are communicators, and we must be effective in order to be successful.

Because we live in a digital age, where text and email have taken over so much, being able to verbally communicate well is sought after. My son once had a girlfriend who, in person, would hardly say a word. But boy oh boy, in a text, she would damn near write a book. She was far more comfortable behind the mask of the text than in person. I need you to be comfortable in person and virtually. In business, you will be required to be personable and communicate effectively in both realms. Your verbal communication is looked at today as a skill and a strength. If you want to learn to be a better verbal communicator, I encourage you to start by listening to some of the great verbal communicators. Our former president, Barack Obama, is an amazing verbal communicator. You can start by listening to some of his speeches. Even if you don't agree with his politics, you can know him for the power in which he speaks. Some other great verbal communicators include Nelson Mandela, John F. Kennedy, Martin Luther King, Jr., and Mahatma Gandhi.

The other way to become a better verbal communicator is to read. Reading was a struggle for a long time for me. I suffer from a minor form of dyslexia. I have an aunt who has full-blown dyslexia. She is unable to read or write. I have worked extremely hard to overcome my disability. I did this by first slowing down. I can move too fast. I learned that I would need to read over things several times to truly understand and comprehend them. I continued to read more and more and actually started to love reading. The more I read, the stronger I became and the less I suffered with comprehension. Imagine that. Practice not only makes perfect, it makes prepared. All the time I spent reading has helped me not only in my ability to read, but also my ability to write. The more I gathered words as I read, the stronger a communicator I became. My vocabulary increased, and even today, I continue to increase my vocabulary.

As speakers, one of the tools we use to help us grow is notecards with words on them. I suggest you give it a try. Just get yourself a deck of index cards. Pull out the dictionary and write the word and definition on the card. Pull out as many words as possible, then practice. Stand in front of the mirror and pull out a card, then create something to say around that word. Repeat as much as you need.

The other way to increase your ability to speak is to get out and start talking to people. As an Empowered Entrepreneur, networking is mandatory. In order to network, you are going to need to be able to communicate.

You will need to communicate your core message regarding your business and your future. You need to communicate in such a way that your audience can understand what you are saying, and that you are able to provide for them what they need. There are many different types of networking events in your local area right now. All you have to do is search for them. If you are in my class at one of the colleges or my virtual course, you will be exposed to many different networking events, and I will ask you to attend a few of them. For now, I want you to find one on your own and go check it out. Just be observant and watch everyone communicating. Then, join in the fun. Make sure to take a business card with you, even it just has your name and contact information on it. Remember, you don't have to have a business or fancy title to have a business card. You just need a name, number, and email. That's it. Your business card will serve as your visual and written communication.

Let's now turn our attention to the final two types of communication: written and visual.

Being a reader, I have already told you, was a struggle for me at first. I literally failed third grade because of it. However, as you see, you are currently reading my first book. I will write at least ten to twenty books in my lifetime. Tell me again I am a failure. I promise I am coming for everything they told me I couldn't have.

Written communication involves anything using the written word to communicate a message. We have vast amounts of written communication. This very book is written communication. In business, you will do a lot of writing. If you struggle with writing, I need you to take a writing course and grow as a writer. As an Empowered Entrepreneur, you are going to need to be an effective communicator, and writing is a large part of business. Written communication is one of the most common forms of business communication in the new millennium and will only increase as we move forward in time. When I first started teaching at the college level, I was absolutely shocked at how many students came out of high school and into college without knowing how to read or write well.

What the hell is really going on? How is it that our education system is failing our students like this? Those were my first questions. My next thought was, *How can I help correct it?* The first thing I did was expose my truth, just as I have done here with you. There is great freedom when we expose our truth because there is always someone in the valley ahead of us that needs our help. They need us to come to them and help raise them up. After that, I told each of my students that I would work directly with them, one on one, to help them become better writers. I gave them tools and tips on how to grow as a reader and a writer. Most importantly, I gave them work to do. Because they are going to have to write, I need them writing well. I am not just building up any type of entrepreneurs, I am building up *EMPOWERED* ones.

We only get better by practice. In order to master something, you must put in at least 10,000 hours. This is true with writing. I am very proud of this book, but the one I will write at my 10,000 mark—oh boy, that one you certainly need to buy. It is going to blow your socks off. Of this I am sure.

So, practice. Learn sentence structure and grammar and the like. The way to start your practice is to journal. Put your pen to paper and just write. Move the self-censoring out of the way and write what comes to you freely. Then go back over it. I still need an editor today. That is perfectly fine. You will want someone to proofread your work. There is nothing wrong with asking for help. Just don't allow others to do all the work for you. Make it a team effort.

The need to develop good writing skills is only highlighted by the fact that, in the new millennium, it is not uncommon to conduct business with customers and suppliers that are established and maintained exclusively through the use of written communications. Let's start with how to properly compose an email. First, you need to remember that you are composing an email, not a text. Text language, such as WYD (what you doing) or LOL (laugh out loud), is not going to work. Please remember that. The following email etiquette tips come from an article written by Vivian Giang, entitled "7 Email Etiquette Rules Every Professional Should Know." These tips originally appeared in Barbara Pachter's book, *The Essentials of Business Etiquette.*

- *"Use a professional email address*
- *Include a clear, direct subject line*
- *Include a salutation when starting an email stream, which can be left out when you are in the middle of a series of emails*
- *Formal: Dear Mr. Smith/Ms. Smith,*
- *Less Formal: Hello, John/Jane,*
- *Use the same sentence structure and paragraphs as in a letter, but you do not need to indent*
- *Try to stay short and to the point*
- *Create an email signature with your contact information, title, etc."*[7]

These tips are a great place to start, but there are some things I need you to remember not to do:

Be cautious when using the "reply all" button. At one of my colleges, the email system defaults to "reply all," and if you don't manually change it, you could easily respond to a group email and send your response to everyone. It can be such an inconvenience, not only to those who receive it, but also to the sender who really didn't need everyone to see their response.

Don't use ALL CAPS—that means you are yelling at someone. Remember, tone is not felt in words that are written. So, if you are trying to crack a joke, it may not be received as funny to the person on the other end. If you are sending something to a group of people, do them a favor and don't expose their email addresses unless it's necessary. Use a BCC, which stands for "blind cc." This way, you send the message to everyone without exposing their email addresses.

You will need to send the email to yourself and then do the BCC for it to work.

The way you compose your email is very important, as well. Below are some examples of what to do and what not to do.

5 Tips for Effective Construction Communication' Kendall Jones, LinkedIn

Outside of emails, you will also need to be able to write memos and business reports. Memos are a little less formal, whereas business reports are more formal. Memos are very short messages. Business reports are four to five pages in length. They are fact-driven and will contain elements of research and a ton of data. They may have some opinions or recommendations, though. Business reports are widely used in corporations and larger-scale businesses. In small business, however, the closest thing to a business report you will ever create is a business plan. We will be heading into the planning section of this book in the next few chapters.

If you are in one of my classes, you will be writing a business plan. I don't believe in the traditional business plan, however, and I will explain why as we move forward. But you will be writing a plan nonetheless. If you are going to be an Empowered Entrepreneur and you are reading this book just to gain greater knowledge, you, too, will need to write out a business plan. If you are not taking one of my classes, I would love for you to join in on one of my courses. You can contact me for more information. My contact information is provided in the front of the book in the Preface, and in the About the Author section in the back. Come join the fun!

I am now going to leave you with some final tips on how to improve your business writing skills. The following tips come directly from an article written by Carolyn O'Hara, entitled "How to Improve Your Business Writing," published in the *Harvard Business Review*.

- "***Think before you write**—Before you put pen to paper or hands to keyboard, consider what you want to say.* [Remember, it is all about the power of your mind. I need you to use all of it. —Natasha M Palumbo]
- ***Be direct**—Make your point right up front. Many people find that the writing style and structure they developed in school doesn't work as well in the business world.* [Learn the language of the business world and use it to your advantage. —Natasha M Palumbo]
- ***Cut the fat**—Read your writing through critical eyes, and make sure that each word works toward your larger point. Cut every unnecessary word or*

sentence. [Remember, less is more. —Natasha M Palumbo]

- **Avoid jargon and $10 words**—*Business writing is full of industry-specific buzzwords and acronyms. And while these terms are sometimes unavoidable and can occasionally be helpful as shorthand, they often indicate lazy or cluttered thinking. Throw in too many, and your reader will assume you are on autopilot—or worse, not understand what you're saying.* [Use your deck of cards. —Natasha M Palumbo]

- **Read what you write**—*Put yourself in your reader's shoes. Is your point clear and well-structured? Are the sentences straightforward and concise?* [Read out loud—it helps you hear what is wrong and what doesn't sound right. —Natasha M Palumbo]

- **Practice every day**—*Writing is a skill and skills improve with practice. Read well-written material every day, being attentive to word choice, sentence structure, and flow."* [8] [Practice makes perfect and prepared. —Natasha M Palumbo]

Merriam-Webster defines **visual communication** as "*any system of signaling in which the signals are received by the eye.*" In other words, visual communication in part or whole relies on eyesight. Visual communication is a broad spectrum that includes signs, typography, drawing, graphic design, illustration, industrial design, advertising, animation, color, and electronic resources.

We are by far more visual communicators in the new millennium than we have ever been before. As an educator, I am always using visual aids. I use PowerPoint slides for almost all of my lectures. They help give my students a better understanding of the information I am lecturing. As a speaker, I even use slides from time to time to help make my presentations more impactful. In business, I use a lot of visual communication. I have been creating flyers and brochures for close to fifteen years. They help me get my message out to potential and existing clients. You will want to ensure you are able to create some clean visuals for your business. Remember, you are *Entrepreneurship Empowered*. The way you communicate should be a reflection of you.

You have now been given information on the four most common types of communication. But I want you to understand that what is most important is how you listen. You must be effective as a communicator to truly be an Empowered Entrepreneur. Effective communication requires you to listen—intently. Do not listen to respond, listen to understand. I started this chapter by telling you about my coach, Kendall Ficklin. I told you one of the things he does that I really love is he shares his conversations with us—the ones he has with potential and existing clients. I learn so much from listening. I am a very observant person. My antennae are all the way up and I am always on the hunt for more knowledge. By listening, I can see things from a different perspective. This is why I tell my students and readers to go listen to some of the great speakers of our day, and even those of the past.

I also encourage you to ask questions when you are speaking with others. It is perfectly fine for someone to repeat something, so you can fully understand them. This means you are listening with the intent to understand. It is also perfectly fine to take notes when you are at a meeting. That way, you can write down important pieces of the conversation. If you take one of my classes at the college or my virtual course online, I will go into more detail on how to be an effective communicator by listening. For now, I want you to keep your ears up and your mind focused when communicating with others. I want you to become a master of communication. You will need to master this in life and in business, regardless of whether or not you are going to be an Empowered Entrepreneur. My goal in the end is to ensure that you are *EMPOWERED!*

According to the National Association of Colleges and Employers, the following are the top five personal qualities or skills potential employers seek:

- *"Communication skills (verbal and written)*
- *Strong work ethic*
- *Teamwork skills (works well with others, group communication)*
- *Initiative*
- *Analytical skills"*[9]

I will share with you a bit later in this book the top ten 21st century soft skills. Communication is on that list as well. It is in high demand because, truth be told, humans are not the best at communicating. If you can become a master at communication, the world is your oyster. To become a master, however, you must again be constantly working on your personal growth in that area.

Emotional intelligence is very important with regard to communication. Have you ever been in a conversation with someone and they have lost control due to their emotions? I believe we all have at some point in our lives. This happens far too often in business as well. This is why having emotional intelligence is so important, especially as an Empowered Entrepreneur. You are going to need to be able to communicate not only with your staff, but with your customers, and you're going to need to understand them—especially from an emotional side.

Communicating via text message or email can make it hard to understand what emotions are at play. Therefore, many conversations are better to have in person or over the phone, so you can see the person's body language or hear their tone. Technology has reshaped the way we communicate, and therein resides an entirely new language itself. You will use your text for business, and you will most certainly use email. Each generation will command you to use a different mode of communication. Again, remember that you are a master and an Empowered Entrepreneur, so you must know how to communicate with all generations on all levels.

"Technology is a useful servant but a dangerous master."

—Christian Louis Lange, historian

Technology seems to be ruling the new millennium more and more. I can only imagine what it will be like in the next century. If we become a servant to it, then it will indeed become a very dangerous master. I want you just to think for a moment about how different careers are now from when they were when you were in grade school. Today, we have drone pilots. Drone data is collected, and it is super rare to find an analyst who can interpret drone data. Those who do are paid very high figures. According to reports from the World Economic Forum and the U.S. Department of Labor, 65% of children who are in grade school right now will be in careers or working in a job that doesn't exist today.[10] Why? Technology, that is why. We will always have technology, and it will only grow. Will it rule our world? Well, to be honest, it already does. It causes more deaths than drinking and driving. It fosters more disconnection than connection. There is more social anxiety now than ever before, and our empathy levels are down. Could it be that we are connected broadly but not deeply?

We need to learn how to work with technology and be the master of it, not the other way around. Knowing how to use your smartphone doesn't mean you know how to work with technology. In *Entrepreneurship Empowered*, you will need to have digital fluency. It is also one of the top 21st century employability skills.

Being able to use your smartphone is of great value. You are able to have a mobile office right there on your phone. However, you also need to know how to use a computer or laptop and understand what hardware and software mean. Hardware consists of the CPU (central processing unit), monitor, keyboard, and other parts you can see and touch. Software consists of the programs, manuals, and procedures that cause the hardware to operate in a desired manner. One of the most important software programs that you should know is the Microsoft Office Suite. It contains Word, Excel, and PowerPoint. I highly recommend you either take a class or watch a YouTube video on how to use all the programs in the Suite. I believe all college students should be required to take a basic Microsoft Suite course because, in college, they will be required to use Word to produce papers, Excel to produce charts and data, and PowerPoint to produce presentations.

Far too many students come to me without knowing how to use any of the Microsoft Suite programs. That is sad. If you don't know how to use Microsoft Suite, please don't do yourself an injustice—go take a course or watch a YouTube video. If you are in my class at one of the colleges or take my virtual online course, you will be required to watch a tutorial on Microsoft Suite and do an assignment with it. Because I am building up Empowered Entrepreneurs, I must ensure I give them all they need to be *EMPOWERED*.

Management information systems (MIS) collect, record, process, report, and/or convert data into a usable form. One of the most important MIS that I used in my business was QuickBooks. There are other valuable MIS software programs on the market. I highly recommend QuickBooks for your accounting needs. 17hats is another wonderful software program that will help keep you and your business organized. *"It is a system that allows you to automate your business processes. It's a tool designed particularly for smaller businesses with fewer staff so that they can manage operations such as billing, scheduling, and meetings, without relying too much on paperwork."*[11]

Adobe is also a must-have. I use it all the time, and I am sure many of you have used Adobe Reader. There are fifteen different programs offered through Adobe. You don't necessarily need all fifteen. Adobe Professional is where I would encourage you to start. I would also encourage you to take a look at their website and review all that they offer for Business Solutions. They have what an Empowered

Entrepreneur needs. All of the software programs we just covered are also available as apps. Even though I don't want you to only depend on your phone, I do understand how important it is to be able to have a mobile office. It is so convenient and efficient.

The internet has just about taken over everything, has it not? Most of all business communication is done via the internet. Many brick-and-mortar businesses offer free Wi-Fi as a way to draw in customers. These days, almost all data reporting, credit card batch processing, and general corporate communication is done online. Almost as important as the internet is the network that supports internet access. Not only does networking connect computers, cash registers, and other essential hardware, but it also provides protection against hacking and data theft. God forbid if the system goes down. The impact is like a ripple effect; it is felt throughout the entire business, and the customer feels it, too. Normally, systems don't take too long to come back up, but for every minute they are down, so is business—so is profit. Have you ever lost all your pictures stored on your phone? I have, and it is crushing.

When systems go down, that same crushing feeling can arise. It is, however, the new millennium, and we are much more protected. We have the cloud.

"The humble Cumulus humilis—never hurt a soul."

—Gavin Pretor-Pinney, author

Cumulus humilis are cumuliform clouds that generally form at lower altitudes. It is almost like you could touch them they are so low. As I mentioned, the internet has become an essential part of business. One of the greatest inventions of the internet is the **cloud**. Cloud computing provides a way for your business to manage your computing resources online.

According to TechTarget, an online technology guide, there are three general cloud deployment models: "*public, private, and hybrid. A public cloud is where an independent, third-party provider, such as Amazon Web Services (AWS) or Microsoft Azure, owns and maintains computer resources that customers can access over the internet. Public cloud users share these resources, a model known as a multi-tenant environment. By comparison, a private cloud is created and maintained by an individual enterprise. The private cloud might be based on resources and infrastructure already present in an organization's on-premises data center or on new, separate infrastructure. In both cases, the enterprise itself owns and operates the private cloud. A hybrid cloud is a model in which a private cloud connects with public cloud infrastructure, allowing an organization to orchestrate workloads across the two environments. In this model, the public cloud effectively becomes an extension of the private cloud to form a single, uniform cloud. A hybrid cloud deployment requires a high level of compatibility between the underlying software and services used by both the public and private clouds.*"[12]

You will want to ensure you do have some way of backing up your information, either via the cloud or in some other form, such as an external hard drive or a flash drive. What I love about Google is that it gives you a cloud space with your Gmail account. You get a certain amount for free, and if you need more, it is available for a small cost. The same is true for your phone.

"Data! Data! Data! I can't make bricks without clay."

—Sir Arthur Conan Doyle, author

Brick by brick—that's how you build a business. Your data, just as the above quote states, is your clay to make the bricks you need to build a business. I couldn't have built my business without all the data from my clients. It was the data they provided me that allowed me to expand into other locations. The virtual world is creating a whole new reality for businesses. The possibilities are endless when it comes to our new virtual world. The internet has made our lives so much easier, and we have a wealth of information at our fingertips.

How do you build an online business, you may be wondering? Building an online business takes more than choosing a brand name, writing product listings, and starting to sell products online. Even the best business ideas can flop if you aren't driving enough traffic to your site. One of the first things you must have is a sharp focus on your target market. You must be as tight with your target market as possible. Amazon.com has thousands of products, this is true, but that is not how it started. It started with a book. So, narrow down your target market and narrow down your products and services. Less is more.

Next, you will need to go through all the steps of the business model and figure out what model works best for you. You will need to ensure you have done all that is required to launch yourself as a business.

Then, move into working on your branding. Social media is one of the best tools to use to build brand awareness. You will want to pick a social media platform to start promoting your business. According to the article "How Consumers Spend Their Time Online" by Connie Hwong, *"Sites and apps like Facebook, Snapchat, and Gmail attract the greatest percentage of consumer online time: 41%."*[13] This is why I say you need to make sure you start promoting your business on social media.

You will want to use social media to build your brand as well—to draw people to your website. Just because you set up a website doesn't mean people will start to flock to your site. That doesn't happen. Online customers are not easier to service either, so go ahead and remove that from your thoughts as well. Privacy is a big issue, and you will need to ensure that your customers' private information is secured.

In order to have a strong web presence, you are going to need a plan. The plan should address issues such as site design and maintenance, creating and managing a brand name, marketing and promotional strategies, sales, and customer service.

Building a website is not overly complicated if you are somewhat tech savvy. There are website builders that work perfectly for building a site. You will need to start by having a domain name. GoDaddy owns the largest share of domain names. You can go to the GoDaddy website[14] and type in the name you want. However, just because you want a name doesn't mean you will be able to get it. Even if you think your name is unique, so did someone else, and they may have gotten to it before you. So, try to be creative and play around with a few different names.

You will find that domain names typically don't cost very much. I have several domain names that I am just sitting on because they were cheap to pick up, and I plan to use them at the right time. GoDaddy also has a built-in template that you can use to build your website. I used GoDaddy to build a nice website for my nonprofit work, the STEEL Legacy. It was super simple to use and very forgiving. However, I am very tech savvy, so it worked for me. If that is not the case for you, then you will want to reach out and find a full-service developer.

When you work with a full-service web designer, they can help you set up everything from a website to helping you with the search engine. In the new millennium, finding a good web designer is not that difficult. A simple search on Google should pull up a nice list for you. Make sure you check out their work and see if you can speak with people who have used their services. Remember, they will only build the site—you will be running the business. You will need to ensure you have some technical skills in order to run an online business, or you will need to have a staff that does.

"The Internet is becoming the town square for the global village of tomorrow."

—Bill Gates, founder of Microsoft

It is amazing to think how far the internet has come since its inception in 1989. The internet was created by a computer scientist by the name of Tim Berners Lee.

Interestingly enough, he worked at the European Organization for Nuclear Research. And, like a bomb, the internet has exploded all over us. Truth be told, we love it. I don't know if we would know how to live without it. At our very fingertips is a wealth of knowledge, our friends and family, news, and all the shopping we want. The internet has truly transformed our lives. I can only imagine how much more it will transform us as we move forward.

I always tell my students that we don't predict the future; we create it. It is true. Technology is one of the largest tools we use to create our future. I can only imagine what it will be like in a hundred years. I started the technology section of this chapter with a profound quote about not allowing technology to be our master, though I am confident it will never hold one of the most unique elements of a human: emotion. I still refuse to ask Siri questions, because I am concerned she is going to tell me her logic is undeniable, and I simply don't have time for any of that nonsense. I am emotionally intelligent, and I plan to stay that way.

Don't let this technology fool you. Technology may be a large tool for creating our future, but our mind is even larger. That is the one thing I want you to continue to develop and build up. You will do so by working with technology, but more so by being a lifelong learner. Knowledge is where the real power lies. Get all you can. This is how you become *EMPOWERED.*

Chapter 3: Types of *Empowered Entrepreneurs*, Business Legal Structures, and Intellectual Property

"Don't worry about being successful but work toward being significant and the success will naturally follow."

—Oprah Winfrey, business tycoon

Entrepreneurship Empowered is more about being significant than it is about being successful. Too many people chase success and, like a puppy chasing its tail, they just go 'round and 'round, never fully grasping it. Those who seek to be significant, to make an impact, they are the ones whose names are remembered and whose faces we will never forget. We find them in our schoolhouses, churches, hospitals, and so on. Just as Oprah tells us in the quote at the top of the page, success will naturally flow when we are striving to be significant. To leave this earth a little better than we found it. Being an Empowered Entrepreneur is such a great calling to pursue. We are the leaders in this new millennium, and you find us everywhere.

Types of Empowered Entrepreneurs

Let us turn our attention to the different types of Empowered Entrepreneurs. There are ***intrapreneurs.*** These are employees of a larger-scale business or corporation that have the ability to create and operate as an entrepreneur. The dictionary defines an intrapreneur as *"an employee of a large corporation who is given freedom and financial support to create new products, services, systems, etc., and does not have to follow the corporation's usual routines or protocols."*

Listen, being an intrapreneur is not a bad gig. Imagine for a moment, if you will, having all the perks of being your "own boss," but someone else cuts you a check and they provide you with benefits, vacations, retirement, and more. Sounds pretty sweet to me. Here are the drawbacks, however. What you invent is not yours—it belongs to the corporation or business and stays with them, should you choose to leave. They own your intellectual property. In the end, you are still working for someone else, building up someone else's business and not yours. You are a free-range chicken on a caged farm.

Franchising is another form of Entrepreneurship Empowered. Franchises are known as turnkey business. Investopedia defines a turnkey business as *"a business that is ready to use, existing in a condition that allows for immediate operation."* Franchise has a language of its own, and if you are interested in buying a franchise or creating a business that you would like to franchise, it is best to seek legal counsel. You will want to make sure they practice franchise law.

The franchisee is an entrepreneur who buys a franchise (business) from the franchisor (business owner). According to the Small Business Administration (SBA), there are two common forms of franchising:

- *"**Product/trade name franchising:** The franchisor owns the right to the name or trademark of a business and sells the right to use that name and trademark to a* *franchisee. This style of franchising normally focuses on supply chain management. Typically, products are manufactured or supplied by the franchisor and delivered to the franchisee to sell.*

- **Business format franchising:** *The franchisor and franchisee have an ongoing relationship. This style of franchising normally focuses on full-spectrum business management. Typically, the franchisor offers services like site selection, training, product supply, marketing plans, and even help getting funding.*"[15]

For many people, franchising works well. It does, however, require you to have a large sum of money and collateral. Franchises will range in price, and the royalty fees will range. To make the wisest investment with regard to a franchise, I highly recommend you work directly with a franchise lawyer or a business consultant who specializes in franchising. As I stated previously, there is a particular language and a ton of paperwork that comes with buying a franchise.

Studies have found that veterans do well owning a franchise. Why do you think that is? They are accustomed to structure and follow orders. Franchises are a perfect fit.

Another way to enter the world of *Entrepreneurship Empowered* is by **buying a small business.** I bought a small business. The risk was fairly low, as that business was well established and I had been working for it for some time. It was certainly much easier than starting a business from the ground up, which I later did as well.

Some challenges one may face when buying a small business include: Will the customers stay? Will they like the new owner? Will the brand stay the same? What will the new service be like? When I purchased my business, Dan asked me not to change the logo. Though I could, of course, he simply asked that I not. He had worked very hard on that logo and was proud of it. I kept it, and to this day, with only a very slight modification to it, I use it with my business. To be honest, I am glad he asked me to keep it. I might have changed it if I weren't staying true to my promise, and by doing so, I could have damaged the brand. My clients know that logo. The hearing offices where I copied knew the logo. I had that logo on everything from stationary to business cards to T-shirts. My clients were used to seeing the logo. They knew it was Start To Finish Files without me having to put my name on it. I had brand recognition with the logo. In branding, your logo is critical to your brand awareness and building recognition of your business. This is why I have an entire chapter of this book dedicated to marketing, branding, and advertisement.

Social entrepreneurs you may not have heard of before. Social entrepreneurs help solve community-based problems and focus on creating positive changes for society. According to *Forbes*, *"Social entrepreneurs play the role of change agents in the social sector by:*

• Adopting a mission to create and sustain social value (not just private value),

• Recognizing and relentlessly pursuing new opportunities to serve that mission,

• Engaging in a process of continuous innovation, adaptation, and learning,

• Acting boldly without being limited by resources currently in hand, and,

• Exhibiting a heightened sense of accountability to the constituencies served and for the outcomes created."[16]

Social entrepreneurs address the wicked problems of the world, such as poverty, homelessness, pollution, and the like. I am a social entrepreneur. The main problem I address is homelessness, which is an epidemic. Mental illness is a major player when it comes to homelessness. Businesses that have a focus on social and environmental issues tend to be much more successful and profitable. Just as I told you in the beginning, if it is about being significant, then success will naturally flow. Social entrepreneurs are all about being significant and making an impact.

Serial entrepreneurs are some of my favorite people because—well, here again—I am one of them. We are habitual entrepreneurs. We are constantly creating businesses. I always joke that even as they are laying me to rest, I will be throwing one more business out of the casket.

Serial entrepreneurs will start businesses one after another, or even several at one time. There really is no rhythm or rhyme to our madness. We just create. Many times, serial entrepreneurs will create a business and then sell it. They don't have much interest in operations or management. Again, they like to create. Other times, they will keep a business or two. The reality with a serial entrepreneur is they are not satisfied with just one business. They are constantly looking to make it bigger or better, or just make something completely new. Mark Cuban, Elon Musk, and Richard Branson, just to name a few, are all serial entrepreneurs.

Now that we have covered a few different types of Empowered Entrepreneurs, I want you to think for a moment about which type of Empowered Entrepreneur you believe you are. Does your mind never shut off, or are you always creating, like the serial entrepreneur? Do you need order and structure? If so, perhaps being a franchisee would work best. What about buying an existing business, how would that suit you? Do you have a heart and a passion for saving the world? Then maybe you are a social entrepreneur. Or do you wish to work inside either a corporation or business and operate in your entrepreneurial gift that way? Take a moment and think. Then, on the lines provided below, write out which Empowered Entrepreneur you believe you are. Knowing this information will be helpful as you move forward in the book.

_____

_____

_____

_____

_____

_____

Business Legal Structures

The way you legally structure your business is a very important step, and far too often, it's done very quickly or even overlooked. I have so many stories from students and clients who tell me how they structured their business as a limited liability company (LLC) and only ended up with a large tax bill. They didn't even generate any profit from their business. What they failed to do was really take time to ask themselves some very important questions.

The first step in structuring your business is to assess your risks. What are they? Could insurance cover low risk? What type of investments do you have that someone could take? Do you need to be an LLC or corporation to get a contract or do a particular type of work? Do you really need to be an LLC or corporation? I need you to think carefully about these questions. The answers will determine how you structure your business. It is critical that you do as much research as possible. Don't make the mistake of choosing the wrong structure. When choosing your business structure, it is wise to consult with a business lawyer or even a tax accountant. Both will help you make a sound decision.

Sole proprietorship is the simplest, most inexpensive, and most common business structure. Sole means one owner. Because the man that owned my business prior was a sole proprietor, I just naturally became one as well. As a sole proprietor, I have no protection. The liability is all mine. That is the most important takeaway for sole proprietorship: you are not protected. Of course, there is insurance to acquire, and we will discuss the different types of insurance a little later in the book.

According to the SBA, *"sole proprietorships do not produce a separate business entity. This means your business assets and liabilities are not separate from your personal assets and liabilities. You can be held personally liable for the debts and obligations of the business."*[15] Just because you begin as a sole proprietor doesn't mean you will stay one. Amazon is a perfect example of a company that started as a sole proprietorship, and now Amazon is clearly ruling the world! Okay, so it's not ruling the world, but it is now a publicly traded corporation.

Sole proprietorship is extremely easy to form. In many areas, there is no legal filing fee at all to be a sole proprietor. If you choose to use a business name, you will need to research your local county's process to file for a DBA, also known as **D**oing **B**usiness **A**s. Your DBA becomes your legal name and you are then able to open a business bank account. My DBA is Start To Finish Files. Having a DBA adds to your professionalism. This doesn't mean you cannot use your name—many people do. The decision is up to you and what works best for your business. Your business may fall in an area or industry that requires licenses or permits. In that case, you will have a small fee to pay and you will need to make sure to keep up with the renewal of those licenses and permits so you don't incur additional charges.

Taxes for a sole proprietorship are simple as well. They are seen as personal taxes. Remember, you and your business are one entity, which means you are together. You will file one tax return, which will lay out your expenses and your income. There is a self-employment tax that you need to be aware of—it is fairly large, and when you first encounter it, it may shock you. You will want to visit the Internal Revenue Service's website and explore the detailed information regarding taxation for sole proprietorship. After all, they are the ones you are paying the money to.

"The best partnerships aren't dependent on a mere common goal but on a shared path of equality, desire, and no small amount of passion."

—Sarah MacLean, author

Partnerships are another way many businesses are structured. Partnerships are two or more people who share in the building of a business. Partnerships are an interesting dance, like the two-step; however, not everyone can do the two-step, nor should they try. Understanding yourself is key to knowing whether or not a partnership will work for you. I

ENTREPRENEURSHIP EMPOWERED

am a controller, so most partnerships do not work for me. I need to be in control and call the shots. I am very comfortable raising people up to lead, as that is part of the business I am in. However, I need them to go lead on another ship, not mine. They come to me to be trained, and I send them out to lead and train others.

Setting up a partnership is simple to do. You don't even need a contract, but I highly recommend that you do have a contract to protect yourself. It must be detailed, and it must hold all relevant information, such as who will be doing what (roles), who will make decisions, who will handle the money, who gets what cut of the money, who will hold the most liability, and how will the business dissolve. There are many templates out there regarding partnership contracts. My advice is to research them and find one that works best for you and your partner(s). You can always edit a template to make it yours. You should also consider taking the document to a lawyer for review—or even have them create one for you. What you don't want to do is go into business with someone regardless of how much you trust or love them, without a written contract in hand.

Have you ever heard of a "silent partner"? Silent partners are found in **_limited partnerships_** (LP). According to the SBA, "_Limited partnerships have only one general partner with unlimited liability, and all other partners have limited liability. The partners with limited liability also tend to have limited control over the company, which is documented in a partnership agreement. Profits are passed through to personal tax returns, and the general partner— the partner without limited liability—must also pay self-employment taxes._"[15]

One example of an LP is a gym. Many times, there are multiple owners in a gym. I was a member of a local gym that was set up as an LP. The staff and members actually loved the silent partner. He would come in from time to time and work on things in the gym, but the general manager was a real jerk. He needed to get off the juice, in my opinion. The general manager made some poor business decisions, but the limited partner, though he didn't agree with the decisions, was not able to change them. He had to remain silent. The problem with an LP is that someone else, just like the gym case given, can make poor business decisions, which ultimately will have a direct effect on the investment of the limited partner. The limited investor could potentially lose their investment, all because of poor management and poor business decision-making.

The reason why someone would choose an LP varies, from lack of managerial skills in the industry (yet money to invest, due to seeing an opportunity for profit and growth) to someone who has been in the industry for many years but has no interest in managing anymore. They just want the investment and they know the game. In the case of the gym, the silent partner had been in the gym business for decades, and he owned several gyms in different locations and sold them off. This particular gym he kept, but only as a silent partner. He allowed the other partner to buy into the business and be the general partner in the partnership.

Again, there is also the **limited liability partnership (LLP)**. According to the SBA, "*limited liability partnerships are similar to limited partnerships but give limited liability to every owner. An LLP protects each partner from debts against the partnership, and they won't be responsible for the actions of other partners.*"[15]

As a final reminder regarding partnerships, you are getting into bed with someone, as they say. Be very cautious. Cover your bases. Make sure everything is in writing and that you have a very clear escape clause. Seek legal counsel. Then go roll around in the hay and see if you can make some magic. With partners, we are stronger. We have combined resources, talents, skills, and abilities. Partnerships are known to have nice business lifespans. When done right, partnerships are the stones on which to build a very secure and stable foundation. Two are greater than one, for they have double the labor. And if either falls, the other is there to pick him or her up.

No on to a **limited liability company** (LLC). According to the SBA website, *"an LLC lets you take advantage of the benefits of both the corporation and partnership business structures. LLCs protect you from personal liability in most instances, your personal assets—like your vehicle, house, and savings accounts—won't be at risk in case your LLC faces bankruptcy or lawsuits. Profits and losses can get passed through to your personal income without facing corporate taxes. However, members of an LLC are considered self-employed and must pay self-employment tax contributions towards Medicare and Social Security.*

LLCs can have a limited life in many states. When a member joins or leaves an LLC, some states may require the LLC to be dissolved and re-formed with new membership— unless there's already an agreement in place within the LLC for buying, selling, and transferring ownership.

LLCs can be a good choice for medium- or higher-risk businesses, owners with significant personal assets they want to be protected, and owners who want to pay a lower tax rate than they would with a corporation."[15]

Today, LLCs seem to be very popular. Many times I have had students and clients come to me who have already formed their business as an LLC. There is a process to filing an LLC—in the Launch, Manage, and Grow chapter of this book, I will provide the steps you need to follow. For now, I just want you to understand that this is a very common form of business, as it does protect the business owner from the business itself. You will certainly want to work with an attorney or lawyer when forming your business if you specifically plan to form yourself as an LLC.

The following information comes directly from the SBA. A ***corporation (C corp)*** is *"a legal entity that's separate from its owners. Corporations can make a profit, be taxed, and can be held legally liable. Corporations offer the strongest protection to their owners from personal liability, but the cost to form a corporation is higher than other structures. Corporations also require more extensive record-keeping, operational processes, and reporting. Unlike sole* proprietors, partnerships, and LLCs, corporations pay income tax on their profits. In some cases, corporate profits are taxed twice—first, when the company makes a profit, and again when dividends are paid to shareholders on their personal tax returns. Corporations have a completely independent life separate from their shareholders. If a shareholder leaves the company or sells his or her shares, the C corp can continue doing business relatively undisturbed. Corporations have an advantage when it comes to raising capital because they can raise funds through the sale of stock, which can also be a benefit in attracting employees. Corporations can be a good choice for medium- to higher-risk businesses, or businesses that need to raise money, and businesses that plan to 'go public' or eventually to be sold.

S corp. An S corporation, sometimes called an S corp, is a special type of corporation that's designed to avoid the double taxation drawback of regular C corps. S corps allow profits, and some losses, to be passed through directly to owners' personal income without ever being subject to corporate tax rates. Not all states tax S corps equally, but most recognize them the same way the federal government does and taxes the shareholders accordingly. Some states tax S corps on profits above a specified limit and other states don't recognize the S corp election at all, simply treating the business as a C corp. S corps must file with the IRS to get S corp status, a different process from registering with their state. There are special limits on S corps. S corps can't have more than 100 shareholders, and all shareholders must be U.S. citizens. You'll still have to follow the strict filing and operational processes of a C corp. S corps also have an independent life, just like C corps. If a shareholder leaves the company or sells his or her shares, the S corp can continue doing business relatively undisturbed. S corps can be a good choice for a business that would otherwise be a C corp, but meet the criteria to file as an S corp.

B corp. A benefit corporation, sometimes called a B corp, is a for-profit corporation recognized in the majority of U.S.

states. B corps are different from C corps in purpose, accountability, and transparency, but aren't different in how they're taxed. B corps are driven by both mission and profit. Shareholders hold the company accountable to produce some sort of public benefit in addition to a financial profit. Some states require B corps to submit annual benefit reports that demonstrate their contribution to the public good. There are several third-party B corp certification services, but none are required for a company to be legally considered a B corp in a state where the legal status is available.

Close corporation. Close corporations resemble B corps but have a less traditional corporate structure. These shed many formalities that typically govern corporations and apply to smaller companies. State rules vary, but shares are usually barred from public trading. Close corporations can be run by a small group of shareholders without a board of directors.

Nonprofit corporation. Nonprofit corporations are organized to do charity, education, religious, literary, or scientific work. Because their work benefits the public, nonprofits can receive tax-exempt status, meaning they don't pay state or federal taxes income taxes on any profits they make. Nonprofits must file with the IRS to get tax exemption, a different process from registering with their state. Nonprofit corporations need to follow organizational rules very similar to a regular C corp. They also need to follow special rules about what they do with any profits they earn. For example, they can't distribute profits to members or political campaigns. Nonprofits are often called 501(c)(3) corporations—a reference to the section of the Internal Revenue Code that is most commonly used to grant tax-exempt status.

Cooperative. A cooperative is a business or organization owned by and operated for the benefit of those using its services. Profits and earnings generated by the cooperative are distributed among the members, also known as user/owners. Typically, an elected board of directors and officers run the cooperative while regular members have *voting power to control the direction of the cooperative. Members can become part of the cooperative by purchasing shares, though the number of shares they hold does not affect the weight of their vote."*[15]

Is your head spinning? Are you still perplexed as to which business legal structure to choose? Don't worry. Business structures have a lot of moving parts. Take my advice and find a small business lawyer to help you. If you don't have the money for legal help, I would suggest reaching out to the closest law school. Many law schools have free law clinics. The students, in my opinion, are fresher than some lawyers, and they are more eager to learn. See what advice they offer you. Deciding your legal structure is very important and you really do need to make the best decision. As I stated in the beginning, you will need to assess your risk and how much you have in assets that could be lost if some legal matter does come up.

You are able to change your business structure along the way, so if starting as a sole proprietor is the wisest choice, then go with it. Then, as you grow in assets and your business grows in risk, you will be able to consider restructuring your business. What I don't want you to do is jump into an LLC, pay large sums of money, and end up on the losing side.

Below, I have provided a chart that lays out all the different types of business structures we just covered:

Business Structure	Ownership	Liability	Taxes
Sole Proprietor	One Person	Unlimited Personal Liability	Personal Tax Only
Partnerships	Two or More People	Unlimited Personal Liability Unless Structured as a Limited Partnership	Self-Employment Tax (except for limited partnerships) Personal Tax
Limited Liability Company (LLC)	One or More People	Owners Are Not Personally Liable	Self-Employment Tax Personal Tax or Corporate Tax
Corporation C – Corp	One or More People	Owners Are Not Personally Liable	Corporate Tax
Corporation S – Corp	One or More People, But No More Than 100, and all must be U.S. Citizens	Owners Are Not Personally Liable	Personal Tax
Corporation B – Corp	One or More People	Owners Are Not Personally Liable	Corporate Tax
Corporation Nonprofit	One or More People	Owners Are Not Personally Liable	Tax-Exempt, But Corporate Profits Can't be Distributed

Created by Entrepreneurship Empowered based on information from the SBA: Business Legal Structures

ENTREPRENEURSHIP EMPOWERED

Intellectual Property

"To achieve patent commercialization success, every inventor must think like a businessman."

—Kalyan C. Kankanala, IP attorney

Each of us has intellectual property (IP). IP is an asset to an individual, and many businesses thrive off of IP. I remember all too well my state job interview. In the third and final interview, I politely stated that I had intellectual property available for lease. The interviewers looked at each other and then looked at me. I am not exactly sure what their thoughts were, but I received a call no sooner than I made it home, telling me I was hired and that I started on the Tuesday following the Labor Day holiday. Boom! I was in, just like that. IP sealed the deal. I gave the state quite a bit of my IP until enough was enough. Now I am very protective of my IP, and you should be as well.

There are four major types of IP:

- A **copyright** gives the creator of an original work exclusive rights to it, usually for a limited time. Copyright may apply to a wide range of creative, intellectual, or artistic forms, or works. Copyright does not cover ideas and information themselves, only the form or manner in which they are expressed. The life of a copyright lasts the lifetime of the artist/author's life plus 70 years.
- A **trademark** is a recognizable sign, design, or expression which distinguishes products or services of a particular trader from the similar products or services of other traders. Trademarks last 10 years and are able to be renewed.
- A **trade secret** is a formula, practice, process, design, instrument, pattern, or compilation of information that is not generally known or reasonably ascertainable, by which a business can obtain an economic advantage over competitors and customers.

There is no formal government protection granted; each business must take measures to guard its own trade secrets (e.g., formula of its soft drinks is a trade secret for Coca-Cola).

- A **patent** is a form of right granted by the government to an inventor or their successor-in-title, giving the owner the right to exclude others from making, using, selling, offering to sell, and importing an invention for a limited period of time, in exchange for the public disclosure of the invention. An invention is a solution to a specific technological problem, which may be a product or a process and generally has to fulfill three main requirements: it has to be new, not obvious, and there needs to be an industrial applicability. The patent will have a life span of 20 years from the filing date.

Just as there are costs to forming your business, there are costs to protecting your IP. You definitely want to hire an attorney who works specifically with IP. Do not risk going to one who doesn't—you may end up not just losing your IP, but a lot of money, too.

We have covered much in this chapter. Lots of terms and definitions. If you attend my class at any of the colleges or if you attend my online course, you will receive even more information, and we will go deeper into all the information covered. I do, however, recommend you read this chapter over a few times to help you digest all the information that has been provided. Remember, knowledge is power. You are going to receive a wealth of information as we move forward. Make sure to mark areas that you would like to go back and reread. Make notes in the margins. Use a highlighter and mark this puppy up. This is no ordinary book. This is your new millennium business guide—it will not only *EMPOWER* you, it will help set you free. Remember, freedom comes in pieces. Let's go get some more!

# Chapter 4: Business Planning

"Organizations are successful because of good implementation, not good business plans."

—Guy Kawasaki, author and entrepreneur

The Empowered Entrepreneur understands that any plan is only black words on white paper, and if not brought to life by DOING, the plan is worthless. I am not a big believer in the business plan. I wrote one business plan in my life. I wrote it while earning my master's degree. By that point, I had already tripled my business. I believe business plans are outdated and irrelevant for today's aggressive and fast-moving market. However, that being said, I do believe in planning. Plans are mission-critical; business plans have a place and time. I will cover both as we move through this chapter. For now, I need you to understand that execution and implementation are the keys to bringing black words on white paper to life. I have read several times that not one single Fortune 500 company started with a business plan.

Not one. I have already told you that as an Empowered Entrepreneur, we create our future; we don't predict it. Business plans are predictions based on historical data. How does that work with a start-up company that has no data? It doesn't. What works are feasibility reports, pitch decks, and the business model canvas.

Planning takes many forms. You may scratch on a Post-it note, an empty envelope, or even a napkin. Yes, you may plan by using thumbnail sketches. If you are artistic in any way, you may actually like this type of planning. You may plan by using a business brief. There is the business model canvas, which we will cover in detail. The feasibility report is another valuable plan. The pitch deck is your showstopper and has been used to secure millions of dollars from investors. And, of course, you have the traditional 28-to-35-page business plan. What is interesting is that the Small Business Administration, which secures and backs 80% of all business loans, has a lean business plan. They, too, have found that having a 28-to-35-page business plan will not work for all.

Because I am a realist, I don't believe that making a student write a business plan in college is the best way to teach the student. I believe in doing pieces of the plan, and even more so, in using the business model canvas as a starting point. Many college students don't have an existing business, so to have them develop a business plan is really a waste of time. The plan they develop just sits on a shelf somewhere, collecting dust—as many plans do—regardless of being created by students or not. What is more relevant is learning pieces of the plan that are important—such as company profile, products and services offered, pricing structure, competencies in computer analysis, marketing, and, of course, financial viability—then being able to take that information and present it to investors and or banks for loans. Presenting is critical.

The social emotional learning piece is more important to me than the writing piece. Not to say that I don't wish to see my students learn how to write because I certainly do, but what I don't want is for them to be able to write a paper but not be able to speak their plan. The power of life and death is in the tongue. Speak your truth. Speak your vision. Speak life.

The pitch deck is a slide presentation that is usually built off of by using the canvas model. It will clearly tell your target audience the key essentials of your business. More importantly, it starts by addressing what the problem is and what solution you have that fixes the problem. There are many templates out there to use, and Guy Kawasaki—the gentleman whose quote started off this chapter—is very well known for pitch decks and has several templates to review and use. Right now, google "Guy Kawasaki pitch decks." You are looking for the top ten slides that Guy recommends you need for your pitch deck. I want you to write those ten slides in the space provided below. Also, be sure to note any other suggestions he has for you regarding the presentation. Then explore the templates he provides, and make sure to save a few for future reference.

ENTREPRENEURSHIP EMPOWERED

The pitch deck is a tool you will use to present as you speak your vision. When you come to your craft with passion and confidence, it will be hard for an investor not to hear you. They may not say "yes" right off the bat, but if you are an Empowered Entrepreneur, you will keep trying. You are gritty.

"A business model really is a system where one element influences the other; it only makes sense as a whole. Capturing that big picture without visualizing it is difficult. In fact, by visually depicting a business model, one turns its tacit assumptions into explicit information. This makes the model tangible and allows for clearer discussions and changes. Visual techniques give 'life' to a business model and facilitate co-creation."

—Alexander Osterwalder, business author

The business model canvas is your new best friend. It starts as a business model, which has four key drivers: the offering, the customers, the infrastructure, and the financial viability.

INFRASTRUCTURE	OFFERING	CUSTOMERS
FINANCES		

Those four key drivers then expand into nine building blocks. Those nine building blocks are the foundation of *Entrepreneurship Empowered.*

What you will see in the next illustration is that the offering is the only thing that doesn't break down. The reason for this is that the offering is what we call in the business world your "purple cow"—it is your value proposition statement. It is what sets you apart from all others. Your infrastructure will break down into three drivers: key partners, key activities, and key resources. Your customers will break down into three drivers as well: customer relationships, customer channels, and customer segments. The base of your model—finances—is broken in half: cost structure and revenue structure.

Key Partners	Key Activities	Value Proposition	Customer Relationships	Customer Segments
	Key Resources		Channels	
Cost Structure		Revenue Streams		

Both images were created by Entrepreneurship Empowered based on Alexander Osterwalder, Business Model Generation

The offering, which is also called the value proposition, is the most important part of your business model. Your job is to provide the most value you can to your customers and clients and the market you serve. You should be offering

ENTREPRENEURSHIP EMPOWERED

better value than your competitors, and you should be able to have sustainability, meaning you must be able to execute on your value for a length of time. The value proposition solves problems and relieves pain. Be sure to ask three questions when defining your business or product:

- *What is the issue I am solving?*
- *Why would someone want to have this issue solved?*
- *What is the underlying motivator for this issue?*

Take a moment now and ask yourself those questions and write down what comes to you.

_____

_____

_____

_____

_____

_____

_____

_____

_____

_____

_____

_____

_____

_____

_____

_____

_____

_____

_____

_____

_____

_____

ENTREPRENEURSHIP EMPOWERED

Now how do we get the job done to solve those problems? Because, in the end, it is about getting the job done. The value you offer is directly tied to getting the job done. Cases will vary from customer to customer and business to business. You will need to understand your customer, who, many times, will let you know what job needs to be done, but whose needs you will also be uncovering. You are going to provide solutions, and you need to remember that your value should be the better solution for customers.

Customers face all kinds of problems in the new millennium. Those problems help guide you in creating solutions. There are four problems that stand out, and if you could address even one of the four, you could be set for life. Those four problems are lack of time, lack of money, lack of skills, and lack of access.

The internet has provided a wagon full of solutions for the lacks listed above. Take access, for example. Say you love Macy's, but you live far away from one. All you need to do is hop on the computer, go to the Macy's website, and shop for as long as your heart desires. You can shop in your pajamas and no one will look at you strangely. You can shop in the middle of the night and no one is going to wonder how you were able to get into the store after closing. The reason is that you brought the store to you. Lack of access—be gone!

The great thing about a business model canvas is that it allows you to easily and draw pictures or words about what your idea entails. It gives you a greater understanding of your business, and it helps develop a process of making connections to your ideas and converting those ideas into a business. It is a very useful tool to lay it all out. Then you develop further—you expand each of the nine building blocks to a deep level, which will help you as you begin to launch or grow your business. But again, remember the plan is no good on paper. You must bring it to life. You must execute the plan.

Let's now turn our attention to the business brief. In my mind, this is the next logical step after you lay out the business model canvas. The meaning of "brief," according to

Webster's Dictionary, is *"short in duration, extent, or length."* So, a business brief is short. It is typically two or three pages. Many times, it may look like an executive summary, but the difference is that the brief will hold more detail than an executive summary. It will also be a bit longer. A typical executive summary is one to two pages in length. The following main points should always be included in your business brief:

- *Company overview*
- *Value proposition*
- *Customer profile and market size*
- *Proof of market demand and potential future growth*
- *Description of team/management and owner experience and education*
- *Actions/goals and milestones met, and those still to be accomplished*
- *Income statement up to three years (projected) and 12-month sales report (projected)*

Most of the time, the business brief is really the only "business plan" you need. It has enough information to get you started and out the door. It is up to you to implement your plans, stay on track with your goals, accomplish milestones, maintain as much control as possible, then stop and reflect on your findings and go re-work your plan for improvement. And the cycle continues.

The feasibility study is used to test the possibilities of a new product, idea, or service. The study will show you if it is feasible for you to pursue the endeavor. A feasibility study could save you a lot of time, effort, and money when done correctly—because if your findings come back that your idea, product, or service is not feasible, you can shelve it until it could possibly be used. Or you could "can it" forevermore. What you don't want to end up doing is pursuing it only to find you have lost a ton of money. It is like climbing the corporate ladder only to discover that you have been climbing for twenty years up the wrong ladder—what a waste. The following elements are important to the feasibility study:

- *Does the idea fulfill a need or solve a big problem?*
- *Is there both a short- and long-term market potential?*
- *Who are the customers, and what are they willing to pay?*
- *Does the opportunity provide competitive uniqueness?*
- *Is the business model feasible (can it be done) and viable (can it be sustainable)?*

The formal study, when fully produced, will have a cover sheet, an executive summary (which you will want to write last), a technical and operational study, and a financial and resource study. You will need to ensure your market research is in there as well. The market research is mission-critical to all plans you put together. You will then close out with a final conclusion.

"Good business planning is 9 parts execution for every one part strategy."

—Tim Berry, business plan author

The business plan is a very traditional, formal plan. One of the first things I want you to understand about writing a business plan is that it is no easy task, and it takes time. If you ever sign up for a class or workshop that guarantees you'll write a money-winning business plan by attending that class or workshop, I need you to walk away. Keep your money and save yourself some time. It is a lie. There is no college class or workshop you can go through and come out writing a plan that is going to land you money. The only way it is possible is if you have somewhat written a plan before. Or if you are a very seasoned and talented writer and researcher. There are hosts of professionals out there, and all they do is write business plans. If you are seeking money and that is what you need the plan for, then go pay to have someone professionally write your plan. However, if you just want to do some planning, the different types listed above are all you need to do. Then take what you have developed and put it into action.

The SBA backs 80% of small business loans. They are not the ones who give the loans out; they only back the loan. The banks are the ones who loan the money to the lender. You must be credit-worthy in order to receive a loan. Please keep in mind, even existing businesses that have been around for many years and have solid statistical data can be disqualified by the SBA. Your chances are much higher if you have excellent credit and your personal and business finances are in good health. *"The SBA requires a personal guarantee from every owner with at least a 20% ownership stake and from others who hold top management positions. A personal guarantee puts you and your personal assets on the hook for payments if your business can't make them."*[15]

I encourage you to go to SBA's website, www.sba.gov, and explore. It is one of your most valuable resources and has a wealth of information.

As I mentioned before, the traditional business plan is 28 to 35 pages in length, plus appendices that include financial statements. The business plan is a series of several different types of analysis. It will have a cover page where the name of the business, the owner's name, and their contact information can be found. The next thing the reader sees is the table of contents. Because business plans are lengthy, the table of contents helps the reader navigate the space. The executive summary is crucial to the business plan and is found directly after the table of contents.

Many people believe you should write the summary last, but when I first started teaching and was required to make my students do business plans, I changed the game. I had them do the summary first, and then they could go back and make changes at the end—if needed. Having them do it at the beginning allowed them to have something to start with. The summary provided them with the starting pieces to work on other sections of the plan. They could take each piece and build upon it. I am not your ordinary professor, and even though I was somewhat bound by what I had to teach, I still turned the tables ever so slightly. It worked.

The executive summary is what catches the reader's attention and gives them enough details, in one or two pages, that makes them want to read more. If the reader's attention is not captivated by the executive summary, they will likely not read any further and toss the plan aside. The summary should *never* be written as an outline. Be creative with it and tell it in such a way that your reader, who, mind you, is your investor, is so excited about you and your business that they are ready to invest that minute. You want to spark something inside of them. Telling your story is a good way to start. Just don't be like a flamingo and run on and on. Tell your story, then come in with your impact. Show them the evidence of your greatest success and most profound impact. Talk about your numbers. Let them dance around ever so gracefully. A little bit from each part of your plan will be addressed in the executive summary. But again, remember to be creative with it and write it so the reader is able to feel your energy through your writing.

The company overview will follow the executive summary. This is where you will find information on the history of the business, as well as its mission, vision, values, and goals. The description of the products or services will be found there. You will even address growth and exit strategies in the company overview.

After the company overview, you will find a series of analyses: industry, market, and competitor. The marketing plan comes next. There are several elements that make up the marketing plan. Make sure you address each one of them. After the marketing plan is complete, it's time to focus on the operational plan. It, too, has several elements that are very important. Then there is a development plan—this can be combined with the operational plan. You may come across some templates that don't have development plans; that is because the elements of the development plan are located in the operation plan.

Then you will move into the final phases of the plan, which consist of the management, the critical risk, the offering, and, most importantly, the financial plan. You will be providing profit and loss statements, balance sheets, sales reports, and the like. Those will all be provided in the appendices. The financial report is a future prediction based on your historical and statistical data—you are now going to plan for the future. Investors are going to want to see numbers that indicate your business will grow—and quickly—and that there is an exit strategy for them on the horizon, during which they can make a profit. Any bank or lender will also ask to see these numbers to make sure you can repay your loan. You need to be realistic with your numbers. Lenders and investors look at plans all the time. They will know when looking at your data if your growth is realistic or not, so be real with them.

The appendices are the final piece of the plan. There is no limit to how my appendices you can have. This is where the business plan could grow quite large. Make sure not to overwhelm the reader, but you don't want them underwhelmed, either.

Remember the story of Goldilocks and the three bears? If you don't know that story, I need you to go read it right now and come back to this book. Goldie just walked in the bear family's house like it was hers. Now there is so much I could say about this story, but the point I want you to take from it is she tried several things while in the bear family's house. All in pursuit of what was just right, just perfect for her. *Not too hot, not too cold. Not too hard, not too soft.* The same principle needs to apply to your appendices. Not too much, not too little. Be Goldie and make it just right. Make it be a perfect fit for you.

There are several different business plan templates on the internet for use. Again, keeping with my Goldie theme, choose which one is just right for you. You will see that, in the new millennium, the leaner version of the business plan is rising to the top. The SBA even has a lean template version on their website, right next to their traditional business plan. The following information comes directly from SBA and is the more formal business plan template.

- "*Executive summary*
  - *Briefly tell your reader what your company is and why it will be successful. Include your mission statement, your product or service, and basic information about your company's leadership team, employees, and location. You should also include financial information and high-level growth plans if you plan to ask for financing.*
- *Company description*
  - *Use your company description to provide detailed information about your company. Go into detail about the problems your business solves. Be specific, and list out the consumers, organization, or businesses your company plans to serve.*
  - *Explain the competitive advantages that will make your business a success. Are there experts on your team? Have you found the perfect location for your store? Your company description is the place to boast about your strengths.*
- *Market analysis*
  - *You'll need a good understanding of your industry outlook and target market. Competitive research will show you what other businesses are doing and what their strengths are. In your market research, look for trends and themes. What do successful competitors do? Why does it work? Can you do it better? Now's the time to answer these questions.*
- *Organization and management*
  - *Tell your reader how your company will be structured and who will run it.*

- o *Describe the legal structure of your business. State whether you have or intend to incorporate your business as a C or an S corporation; form a general or limited partnership; or if you're a sole proprietor or LLC.*
- o *Use an organizational chart to lay out who's in charge of what in your company. Show how each person's unique experience will contribute to the success of your venture. Consider including résumés and CV's of key members of your team.*
- **Service or product line**
  - o *Describe what you sell or what service you offer. Explain how it benefits your customers and what the product lifecycle looks like. Share your plans for intellectual property, like copyright or patent filings. If you're doing research and development for your service or product, explain it in detail.*
- **Marketing and sales**
  - o *There's no single way to approach a marketing strategy. Your strategy should evolve and change to fit your unique needs.*
  - o *Your goal in this section is to describe how you'll attract and retain customers. You'll also describe how a sale will actually happen. You'll refer to this section later when you make financial projections, so make sure to thoroughly describe your complete marketing and sales strategies.*
- **Funding request**
  - o *If you're asking for funding, this is where you'll outline your funding requirements. Your goal is to clearly explain how much funding you'll need over the next five years and what you'll use it for.*

- o *Specify whether you want debt or equity, the terms you'd like applied, and the length of time your request will cover. Give a detailed description of how you'll use your funds. Specify if you need funds to buy equipment or materials, pay salaries, or cover specific bills until revenue increases. Always include a description of your future strategic financial plans, like paying off debt or selling your business.*
- **Financial projections**
  - o *Supplement your funding request with financial projections. Your goal is to convince the reader that your business is stable and will be a financial success.*
  - o *If your business is already established, include income statements, balance sheets, and cash flow statements for the last three to five years. If you have other collateral you could put against a loan, make sure to list it now.*
  - o *Provide a prospective financial outlook for the next five years. Include forecasted income statements, balance sheets, cash flow statements, and capital expenditure budgets. For the first year, be even more specific and use quarterly—or even monthly—projections. Make sure to clearly explain your projections and match them to your funding requests. This is a great place to use graphs and charts to tell the financial story of your business.*
- **Appendix**
  - o *Use your appendix to provide supporting documents or other materials that were specially requested. Common items to include are credit histories, résumés, product pictures, letters of reference, licenses, permits, patents, legal documents, permits, and other contracts.*"[15]

To write or not to write a business plan is really up to you. Remember that if you are seeking a bank loan, you will most definitely need to write a business plan. If you are starting a business, however, you will need to use the business model canvas to help you develop, and then you are going to need to get to work.

The reality is that you need to have already been working. It is in the work that the plan arises. It is in pursuit of our dreams that we give birth to them and make them a reality. There must, and always will be, a call to action in *Entrepreneurship Empowered.* You can never just plan and sit there and see if the words come to life. If you are going to be an Empowered Entrepreneur, you are going to have to do more than just plan. Because I am a LION and I run this jungle, I stay working, and I also continuously adjust the plan. I plan in small pieces. I highly suggest you do the same.

This is the reason why I love the business model canvas so much. It is perfect for a business at any level, from start-up to success. It is just enough planning to get you started. Then, you must go do it. I started the chapter off with a quote that speaks to the importance of implementation. No matter how much planning you do, it is wasted if you don't implement it. This is true with everything that we plan for in our lives. If you have a goal, you must put action behind that goal for it to come to fruition. Are you willing to put in the work required to bring your plans and goals to life? Are you up to the challenge? Or will your plan just sit and collect dust? It is up to you. *The way out is within.*

 **Chapter 5**: Marketing and Branding

"It is very important to understand that emotional intelligence is not the opposite of intelligence, it is not the triumph of heart over head—it is the unique intersection of both."

—David Caruso, actor

Don't make marketing, make magic. Why do I say that, you ask? Well, because really good marketing is the best magic act you will ever see. You know how magic taps into our emotions? Well, that is what really good marketing does, too. Marketing should be tightly wrapped with emotional intelligence. Those who use emotional intelligence within marketing and business have great success and certainly greater profit. Take, for example, Proctor and Gamble (P&G). Their marketing team is absolutely genius with the use of emotional intelligence. During the World Olympics, they ran an ad that focused not on the star athletes, but rather the mothers. Mind you, the mothers are the target market for P&G. They are the buyers. The ad showcased how the mothers have always been there, taking the young athlete to practices, kissing their forehead after a bad game or poor performance, waving flags and cheering from the sidelines as the winning shot was scored. The entire time the ad was running, the most magical music played ever so softly in the background. Then, right as the ad came to a close, the most beautiful words appeared on the screen: **THANK YOU, MOM...** According to IGM Bizcuit, *"this one ad caused the brand attractiveness to grow by over 10%, and within a 17-day period of time the ad raked in 130 million dollars in sales."* Emotional intelligence is critical to marketing. If I am able to tug at your emotions, you had better believe I will easily grab your wallet with the best magic act on the strip.

Marketing is one of my favorite pieces of the business puzzle. Marketing really isn't just one piece to the puzzle, either. It is several pieces. I see it as the border. You know how important the border is to a puzzle, right? Many people build the border first, then move on to filling in the other pieces to reveal the entire picture. Marketing is your border.

In *Entrepreneurship Empowered*, you must have a solid marketing plan. You will need to do market research and be wise in how you choose to brand your business. Your brand is your calling card, and you want to ensure the call is able to get through at all times. At no point should we be hearing you say, "Can you hear me now?" We must always be able to hear you. Your greatest marketing tool is word of mouth (WOM).

This takes me right back to emotional intelligence and its importance. You must be able to connect and relate to your customer or client. You must have empathy. Even more importantly, you must be making sure the job they need you to do is being done properly and in such a way that they have to tell everyone they know all about you and your business. The growth I saw in business was a direct result of WOM. Even today, the reasons my classes fill up so fast is because of WOM. The reason this book will be flying off the shelves is because of WOM. The reason your business will boom is also because of WOM. So, understand how important WOM is, and be sure to include it in your marketing plan.

How do you build successful WOM marketing? You start with a foundation made of solid trust, commitment, and customer satisfaction. You make sure your customers or clients have some of your swag. T-shirts, coffee cups, pens, note pads...anything you can give to them to use which showcases your brand. Another way is to give a referral discount for sending new customers or clients your way. *"Bring a new customer and receive 10% off your next order!"* Or, better yet, give something away for FREE for the referral. According to academic research and Jonah Berger's bestselling book, *Contagious: Why Things Catch On,* there are six key factors that drive what people talk about and share. They are organized in an acronym called STEPPS, which stands for:

- *"Social Currency—the better something makes people look, the more likely they will be to share it*
- *Triggers—things that are top of mind (i.e., accessible) are more likely to be tip of tongue*
- *Emotion—when we care, we share. High-arousal emotions increase sharing*
- *Public—the easier something is to see, the more likely people are to imitate it*
- *Practical Value—people share useful information to help others*
- *Stories—Trojan Horse stories carry messages and ideas along for the ride"*[17]

If you recall the Muhammad Ali quote I left you with in Chapter One, it closes with *sting like a bee.* Well, in WOM, part of your goal is to create a BUZZ like a BEE. This is where your marketing message is amplified by the public. Create an excitement around your product or service. Social media is one of the best tools out there to create such a buzz. As we move forward in this chapter, we will cover marketing and social media in depth. Before we do that, however, we will go into the basic principle of marketing.

When we look at marketing, the basic principle that arises is commonly known as the 4 Ps: *Product, Price, Promotion, and Place*. The model that is a better fit for *Entrepreneurship Empowered*, however, is the **S.A.V.E** model: *Solution (Product), Access (place), Value (price), and Education (promotion)*. From this point forward, I want you to understand that your product or service is the solution. My slogan for STFF for many years has been *"The Better Solution."* This saying is also my personal mantra. There is always a better solution. Period. Do not get all caught up in the features of your product or service; instead, get caught up in solving the problem for your customer or client. You are there to meet their needs—remember that. How easily accessible your business is to your target market is so very important. Remember in the previous chapter when I stated that one of the problems consumers face is lack of access? I gave the example of Macy's and online shopping. You need to be aware of how quickly your target market can access your business not only for the product and or services you provide, but also for the customer support. The access approach looks at how the customer first hears about your business to when they make their first purchase. I promise you that customers and clients care very much about how receptive you are to their feedback, and how available you are to support them.

Value, value, value. It is always about value and so very little about price. People pay for value. Time and time again, studies show that if people see value—even perceived value—they will normally pay whatever you are asking. You must be diligent in showcasing your business value. Your purple cow must be on full display at all times because your value sets your price.

Education brings it home with our **S.A.V.E** model. As an educator, I love this new approach. Provide for your customer or client with the most up-to-date information possible regarding your product or services. Make sure what you share with them is relevant. Have case studies and testimonials ready to share. Be able to show how your solution worked for others in the past. Case studies often show the benefits of using certain methods that are in alignment with your product or services. People are looking for proof. One of the things I share with my students on the first day of class is a book of my life's work. It shows all the different ads I ran, as well as my different marketing materials. I show the original purchase agreement between Dan and me. I show all my businesses over a period of time. I also include several testimonials. Why do I share this book with them? Because it is proof of my work. It is evidence. I am not just talking the talk; I am walking the walk, and, in their hands, they see my footprints. I am an educator. As an Empowered Entrepreneur, you, too, are an educator. Educators come with proof.

Market research is a super important step. So, how do you begin to do market research? Market research is the gathering and interpretation of data in a specific industry. It also includes answers to a series of questions and, more importantly, the development of your target market. There are two types of data that exist for market research: primary data and secondary data. Primary data is data you develop. You gather the information from doing research, test markets, surveys, focus groups, and so on. Secondary data is data that already exists. The research has been done for you and the information is published and available for use. There can be a cost associated with some secondary data, but overall, there is an incredible amount of solid secondary data that is available for free. As with any data, please be sure you check your sources. Make sure the sources are legitimate and reputable. Some of the information that you should be able to find out directly from secondary data is:

- *The total size of your industry*
- *Trends in the industry—is it growing or shrinking?*
- *The total size of your target market and what share is realistic for you to obtain*

- *Trends in the target market—is it growing or shrinking? How are customer needs or preferences changing?*

Below are a few additional questions that you should be able to answer from your research.

- *Who are your customers?*
- *What do they buy now?*
- *Why do they buy?*
- *When do they buy?*
- *What will make them buy from you?*

Who are your customers? This is one of the most important questions to answer. This is also known as your *target market.* I am always reminding my students and clients that they cannot serve everyone, nor do they really want to. Even though I do all I can to drill this into their heads, I always receive in my students' business briefs a very large target market. Then I remind them once again that they must bring in that market and be more focused. The market is broken down into segments. There several different segments, but according to Active Marketing, an online branding and marketing research company, the list below contains the most common. Remember, you will not choose all of them. You will, however, select some.

- "***Psychographic:*** *Grouping your customers into cultural clusters, social status, lifestyle, and personality type.*
- ***Decision Makers:*** *Grouping your customers based on who decides to purchase your product within the company structure.*
- ***Behavioral:*** *Grouping customers by product usage. For example; light, medium, or heavy users. This stage also factors in brand loyalty and the type of user.*
- ***Geographic:*** *Grouping customers by a specific area, such regions of the country or state and urban or rural.*

- **Distribution:** *Grouping customers based on where they go to purchase your product, such as online, store, or through a catalog.*
- **Demographic:** *Grouping customers by age, income level, gender, family size, religion, race, nationality, language, etc."*[18]

I would now like you take a moment and start working on defining your target market. On the space provided below, write out as much detail as you can regarding your target market. Remember to use the list provided above to help you develop your target market. One of the things you will want to consider is, do you have a product or service that is a niche? A niche market is defined as *"a small, more narrowly defined market that is not being served well or at all by mainstream product or service marketers."* I have a niche market: I only serve social security and disability lawyers. Because of my niche, I was able to have somewhat of a monopoly in my industry. Niches are wonderful if you do have one. Take a few moments now and write what comes to you regarding the details of your target market.

_____

_____

_____

_____

_____

_____

_____

_____

_____

_____

_____

_____

_____

_____

_____

_____

The marketing plan contains the competitors analysis. You will need to ensure you do research and find out who your competitors are. You will have competitors, so don't get it in your head that you will not. I had competitors. Even though they were not direct competitors because they were medical record copy services and I was a social security disability records copy service, they were competitors, nevertheless.

In *Entrepreneurship Empowered*, we collaborate more than we compete. Keep that in mind when you are researching your competition. Could they end up being someone you work directly with to grow and build the business? It took some time before I had a direct competitor. His name was Tony. He showed up on the scene, and I promise you, he pissed me off by arriving. I can clearly remember seeing his business card at one of the federal hearing offices I served. I took that business card, tore it apart, and threw in the garbage. I thought to myself, *Who the hell does this guy think he? Trying to come in and take a slice of my pie? Not today, buddy, not today and not ever!* Fast forward to today: Tony sends me checks on a regular basis. The scanning equipment I have today is from Tony. Tony had one thing going for him—okay, two things. First, Tony was Italian like me, and second, Tony was scanning while I was still copying records. He was ahead of the curve, and I needed to be there with him. We joined forces and created an alliance and have been the best of competitors ever since. Collaboration.... Italiano style.

"If you form a strategy without research, your brand will barely float—and at the speed industries move at today, brands sink fast."

—Ryan Holmes, entrepreneur

The marketing strategy process starts with the company vision. The vision of the company addresses the question, "Where is the company going?" It addresses future goals and milestones yet to be accomplished. The mission of the company addresses the following questions: Why does the business exist? What do we do? How do we do it? And for whom do we do it? Both the vision and mission provide direction for the company. Objectives are then set in place, which provides us with the steps on how we are going to get where. We say, "We desire to be..." followed by the steps we must take in order to fulfill our mission. For many years, marketing objectives have been known by an acronym called SMART: **S**pecific, **M**easurable, **A**chievable, **R**ealistic, and **T**ime-based. But it is a new millennium, and we need to be SMARTER, so I have added two more objectives: **E**xecutable and **R**elevant.

At one point in my life, I weighed over 300 pounds. My vision was to be a normal body weight and, above all, healthy. That is where I was going. My mission was to embody a healthy lifestyle in pursuit of my vision. I tried to lose weight many times being SMART, but then I finally became SMARTER. I want you to be a SMARTER entrepreneur, as well. I realized the objectives and critical steps I had to take to achieve my mission, and ultimately, the vision was every day. I needed to do a series of things that cultivated my new chosen lifestyle. I had to prep my food and eat the prepped food. I had to increase my water intake. I had to go to the gym. I had to do all of those steps consistently in order to achieve the results I desired. After a little over a year of discipline, staying focused on my vision, being true to my mission, and following the objectives I had laid out, I achieved one of my health goals of losing over 100 pounds. This is how the marketing strategy works. This is how many things in life work—systems, strategy, and discipline.

I want you now to take some time to think about your vision, mission, and objectives. I would even encourage you to do a little searching on the internet and read some of the top Fortune 500 companies' vision and mission statements. Then go check some small business websites and see what they have as theirs. Do the companies embody their vision and mission statements? Do you see them achieving goals, and are their objectives working? After you have done this little mini-research, I want you to come back to this book and write out your vision and mission statement. I also want you to include some values and goals. Then I want you to write out your objectives. What steps do you need to take in order to reach your vision and fulfill your mission? Use the space provided to develop those steps.

_____

_____

_____

_____

_____

_____

_____

_____

_____

_____

_____

_____

_____

_____

_____

_____

_____

_____

_____

_____

_____

_____

_____

_____

_____

_____

ENTREPRENEURSHIP EMPOWERED

The marketing concept is also very important to understand. There are three components to the marketing concept: customer orientation, service orientation, and profit orientation. The **customer orientation** is all about finding out what the customers want and like, and then providing it to them. In *Entrepreneurship Empowered*, the ability to find out what the customer wants has increasingly become easier. I can almost guarantee that you have some type of rewards card. Whether it is from a grocery store, drugstore, or you simply put your number into a system to collect points, we all have some type of rewards card. Well, these lovely rewards cards are tracking our every purchase. The data that is collected from the use of the reward card gives a company very important information. It now knows what we like, how often we use products, and so on. The company will now send you coupons for a selected set of items they know you are going to buy. Brilliant!

Another way customer orientation is done is by conducting surveys. Surveys provide valuable information. Companies use surveys all the time to not only provide customers with what they want, but also to improve service. **Service orientation** is making sure everyone in the organization is committed to customer satisfaction. I started off this chapter by telling you how *marketing* is a magic show, and that the greatest marketing tool you have is word of mouth—WOM. Service orientation is your key driver for WOM. You need everyone show-ready at all times. I am very customer service focused. It is truly a part of my purple cow, my value proposition. I stand out when it comes to customer satisfaction. Because of my servant's mentality, I have been able to take little and make it much. I have been able to grow in locations, clients, and students, all because I know how important it is to provide excellent customer service. My clients and students, in turn, spread the word about me, and I grow again. Focusing on both customer orientation and service orientation is mission-critical to the success of your business, and it is the only way to be a leader in entrepreneurship in the new millennium.

Profit orientation focuses on the goods and services that will earn the most profit. This was the McDonalds' strategy when they first began. The McDonald brothers realized that what was selling and making the most profit were burgers, fries, and a drink. They eliminated everything else and focused just on that. It worked, and today, McDonald's is a billion-dollar business. This case is just one example, out of a million, of how to use a profit orientation. The key is to focus on what is selling and earning the most profit. Those are the items you want to push.

Many times, people try to do too much. In the United States, we are always about overstuffing our faces. Fill that plate right up with as much as you can. As if you will starve if you only eat a small portion! That is so far from the truth, it is not even funny. Many times, if your plate is too full, you end up wasting the food—or even worse, stuffing yourself until you can hardly breathe and wonder why you keep gaining weight. *Entrepreneurship Empowered* is all about being lean. Keep that in mind as you look at your product and/or services. Do you really need all of them? Are they all making you money? Get rid of something and see how that works. You can always bring it back if you need to. But you cannot get back the lost time and money you spend on trying to sell something that no one wants to buy.

"All of us need to understand the importance of branding. We are CEOs of our own companies: Me Inc. To be in business today, our most important job is to be head marketer for the brand called You."

—Tom Peters, author, in *Fast Company*

Branding is defined by the business dictionary as *"the process involved in creating a unique name and image for a product in the consumers' mind, mainly through advertising campaigns with a consistent theme. Branding aims to establish a significant and differentiated presence in the market that attracts and retains loyal customers."*

I need you to understand that your brand is a promise to your customers, letting them know what they can expect from your offering and how it is different from others. Your logo is the face of your brand. It is part of how you will communicate your brand message, and it should be seen everywhere to grow brand awareness.

The business dictionary defines brand strategy as "*the long-term marketing support for a brand, based on the definition of the characteristics of the target consumers. It includes an understanding of their preferences, and expectations from the brand.*" This brand message will be seen through ads, distribution, and packaging. Two of the most powerful and classic brands are Coca-Cola, which has managed to differentiate itself from other sodas through its consistent strategic branding, and Nike, which involves famous athletes as part of its branding strategy. If you take one of my classes, I will share more with you about the Nike and Coca-Cola brands, as well as the brilliance behind PG&E.

"It's all in a name." Have you ever heard that saying before? Well, it is often true. If you recall me telling you about my business and how I had to have that glorious name *Start To Finish Files*—just like Ray Kroc had to have *McDonald's*. For me, STFF is exactly who I am; I finish what I start.

When you are creating your brand name, you need to be cautious of a few things. First, does someone else already have that name, and are they doing business under that name? You will need to find that out right away. But how do you even come up with a name in the first place? I would encourage you to go to a quiet place, a place that works with your highest element—water, fire, air, or earth. Sit in that quiet place and allow whatever to come to you regarding your business and name. Write down everything that comes. Don't throw anything away at first. Then go back through your list and examine what you have. But don't be too harsh on yourself. Don't judge too much. Just remember a few golden rules.

Have you ever seen the name of a business and thought, *Huh? How do you pronounce that? What does that mean?* You don't want a name that is too confusing, hard to spell, or hard to pronounce. It should not have any underlying message that only you know. It needs to be fresh and timeless because you will want it to be with you the entire time you are in business. Developing a solid brand name is very important. There is power in a name, so choose wisely. I have provided space for you to work on your name. Remember, just let everything come to you, without self-censoring.

A New Millennium Business Guide from Start Up to Succession

There are steps to building your brand. You will certainly need a logo. Many times, the logo is all we see. Take, for example, Starbucks. If you look at most of their products, their name is not on it, just their logo. The same is true with their storefront and store signs. Their logo has gained enough awareness that we know the little funny-looking mermaid lady in a circle is Starbucks. We don't quite know why that is their logo and what it has to do with coffee, but we recognize it, nonetheless. It is unique, and it has been undoubtedly instrumental to the success of the brand. Your logo could start off with your name on it, as Starbucks' did, but any good logo will eventually hold ground with no name needed. That is called brand awareness. The evolution of the Starbucks logo went from having the name on the logo, as well as the language coffee, tea, and spices, and then it changed to just coffee. Then, finally, nothing. No name, no product. Just that funny-looking mermaid.

To go along with your logo, you will want to create a tagline, also known as a slogan. One of the more well-known taglines is Nike's *"Just Do It."* This tagline has been around since the late 1980s. Talk about power in a slogan! Let's now have a little fun. Below are some well-known taglines. Take a moment to read them over and see if you can figure out the company they belong to.

Kid Tested. Mother Approved.
Life's Good
Trusted Everywhere
Maybe She's Born With It
We Try Harder
Keep Walking
Gather 'Round the Good Stuff
Makes Mouths Happy
Something Special in the Air
It's Not Just a Job, It's an Adventure!

How do you think you did? The answers are in the back of the book. Don't cheat and look if you didn't try. But if you did try, look now to see how you did. You might surprise yourself. That is how the programming of marketing works. The essence of your brand message is found in the tagline, and that is why it must be short, simple, clear, and, most of all, memorable. It may be difficult to do, but I am sure you can do it. For my business STFF, my tagline is *"The Better Solution."* I can promise you that I am always looking for better solutions. Not only do I look for them, but I provide them. My tagline is living, and yours should as well. In just a few moments, I am going to share with you my personal tagline and ask you to create one for yourself.

Once you develop your logo and your tagline, you need to put those suckers on everything possible. You should have it on letterheads, envelopes, business cards, flyers, promotional pens, note pads, T-shirts, all packaging...the list goes on and on. Then make sure all your clients receive something from you with your logo on it. My STFF logo was on everything—from the fax order form to the packaging label to the Post-it note inside on top of the file to the bright yellow invoice. I even had T-shirts made that my staff and I wore and that I would give to my clients when I came around and visited them. I am big on branding. Part of your brand is also your appearance. Today, I am known for my shoes: high heels. It is part of my brand. I am also known for snapping my fingers. I snap—ergo, Snap Queen! That, too, is a part of my brand.

There are many things that contribute to your brand and the awareness your brand attracts. Make sure you take the time to develop your brand and remember to always deliver on your brand promise. Rules were meant to be broken, but promises were not. Keep your word and keep your promise.

You are the brand. Right now, I am going to give you a self-branding assignment. I promise it will be a lot of fun. I want you to ask five to seven people to describe you in three words. Tell them that you will not be upset by what they say if they did need to say something that could be a little hard to swallow. You need to know. Tell them not to think very long but say whatever three words come to mind. Make sure you write them down. If you see a word pop up more than once, make sure to circle that word. It may happen with a few words. Then you are going to reflect on what you have been told. The words that popped up a few times are your strongest brand traits. Now, do you agree or disagree with the way you were described? Write about it.

How people see you is your brand. You need to be aware of how you are being seen. The next part of this assignment is to create a mantra or tagline. A mantra is short and to the point. This mantra is for your life. Not for a business, but for you. The next step is to create a logo. Design yourself a personal logo. I am going to provide you my examples of how I did this assignment, and then there will be space provided for you to write your answers. You may also want to use a computer to do this work.

Self-Branding Assignment example:

- Words that describe me:
  - Creative, Bold, Giving
  - Giving, Passionate, Leader
  - Bold, Driven, Gritty
  - Aggressive, Brave, Creative
  - Strong, Giving, Leader
  - Passionate, Bold, Driven
  - Resilient, Gritty, Giving
    - ➢ I would have to agree with the words that others have used to describe me. I know some of my core strengths are being a leader, creative, and I love to give. I can be aggressive from time to time, but I would hope others would not be too taken aback by my aggressive traits.
- Mantra/Tagline:
  - Empowered Encourager

○   Logo:

A New Millennium Business Guide from Start Up to Succession

"Social media is changing the way we communicate and the way we are perceived, both positively and negatively. Every time you post a photo or update your status, you are contributing to your own digital footprints and personal brand."

—Amy Jo Martin, author

I mentioned at the beginning of the chapter that we would go into how to market on social media in depth. Well, here we are. Did you know you leave a digital footprint almost everywhere you go? Well, online, that is. It is so important for you to watch what you post. Because it can and will be used against you. This is why you must stay focused on promoting yourself well on any and all social media platforms. You will certainly need to be able to use social media to do some of your marketing. I am public on my Instagram. You may follow me there if you don't already: Natasha M Palumbo. I am me being me and being my brand. I use it to promote my businesses and my show my life. I have all my posts on there. You can see my evolution in my business, my weight loss, the colleges I teach at, and my current creations. I am an Empowered Entrepreneur who shares herself with the world.

I went public in June of 2018. At that time, I had just about 200 followers. I started working with a branding and social media expert: Nicky Saunders, CEO of Beast Mode Digital. You may contact her at nicky@beastmode-digital.com for more information. She immediately gave me tools and so much value. I mean, her purple cow was amazing! With her advice and recommendations—and my hard work—my following began to grow and continues to grow daily. In my first month of being public, I grew 100%. Each month after, the growth continues to be very high. How do I do that, you ask? I use hashtags. The hashtag game is incredible. It works only with Instagram and Twitter. I create beautiful content, and I post often (three times a day, if not more). Every time I post, I make sure I use hashtags. There are hashtag apps out there that help you generate hashtags. You just put your topic word in and click "search."

There are many different types of social media out there. It is up to you to figure out which one will work best for you and your target market. You also need to understand that it takes work to manage your social media for your business, and you may need someone to help you with that. You don't need all social media platforms. Again, I use what works best for me—with Instagram being my favorite of all. However, I do have a Facebook page: *Entrepreneurship Empowered*. I hope you will connect with me there and become a part of our community. I don't currently have a Twitter account, and I'm not sure I will get one. I don't do Snapchat, but I might have to get one because the filters are amazing! I am building my LinkedIn profile so it can be of better use to me. It is a professional social media site. I have a LinkedIn expert I work with, and I even bring him to my classes to guest speak from time to time. His name is Robert T. "YB" Youngblood. I recommend connecting with him. His information is YB@YourLinkedInLocksmith.com. You may also connect with him on LinkedIn.

I have now given you two experts that I highly recommend and trust. It is important to take advantage of working with an expert. You normally only have to get with them two or three times to get what you need. It will be up to you to use the wisdom and expert advice they give you. I can attest in advance that it works when you work it.

Now we need to bring all our pieces together and put them into a marketing plan. I have provided a simple marketing plan below, which I suggest you use to do some developing of your own. The following information is from the SBA and is the most common marketing template information in the new millennium.

- *"**Target market**
    - *Describe your audience in detail. Look at the market's size, demographics, unique traits, and trends that relate to demand for your business.*

- *Competitive advantage*
  - *Describe what gives your product or service an advantage over the competition. It might be a better product, a lower price, or an excellent customer experience. Sometimes, an environmentally friendly certification or 'made in the USA' on your label can be an important factor for customers.*
- *Sales plan*
  - *Describe how you'll literally sell your service or product to your customers. List the sales methods you'll use, like retail, wholesale, or your own online store. Explain each step your customer takes once they decide to buy.*
- *Marketing and sales goals*
  - *Describe your marketing and sales goals for the next year. Common marketing and sales goals are to increase email subscribers, grow market share, or increase sales by a certain percent.*
- *Marketing action plan*
  - *Describe how you'll achieve your marketing and sales goals. List marketing channels you'll use, like online advertising, radio ads, or billboards. Explain your pricing strategy and how you'll use promotions. Talk about the customer support that happens after the sale. The federal government regulates advertising and labeling for a number of consumer products, so make sure your advertising is legally compliant.*
- *Budget*
  - *Include a complete breakdown of the costs of your marketing plan. Try to be as accurate as possible. You'll want to keep tracking your costs once you put your plan into action."*[15]

Marketing is a very large topic and contains vast amounts of information. I could write an entire book on it—and just may one day—but for now, here is where I leave you with marketing. It is critical to your business. It would be wise to take advantage of experts, as I have stated above. You will not want to rush through marketing research or the planning of it. You need to take your time. Marketing will need to be managed, just like many other things in your business. Be sure to reflect. Make changes and adjustments when needed. Logos and slogan designs are so great for marketing because once you have them, there will be few changes needed. For all other aspects of marketing, there will need to be adjustments made as you move forward in the future. We are *Entrepreneurship Empowered*. Our brand must carry that essence. If not, it will get left behind in the Dark Ages.

**Chapter 6**: Financial Planning, Accounting, and Funding Your Business

"It's not how much money you make, but how much money you keep, how hard it works for you, and how many generations you keep it for."

—Robert Kiyosaki, author

Robert Kiyosaki is the author of *Rich Dad, Poor Dad*. He explains in his book that the wealthy have a language of their own. They understand the true meaning of assets and liabilities. I always share him with my students. He holds a key that I need each of them to have. I would like to share that key with you all now: "*Pay yourself first.*" That is the key. It requires self-discipline. It is not easy to pay yourself first. Especially when the bills are due, the rent needs to be paid, you need food to eat, and so on. Of course, you want to make sure you take care of your need to live—please don't get me wrong—but far too often, people don't have a money problem, they have a spending problem. People are wasteful with their money. It is not your salary that makes you rich, but rather your spending habits. I make all my students track their money. This is one of the best ways to figure out what is really going on with your finances. The longer you can track, the better. I have my students track for two weeks, but if you can track for a month up to three months, you will have some good data to see what is really going on with your money. You must track it to the penny. Always keep a little book with you and don't miss one cent. Seriously, to the penny.

Once you have tracked your money for a period of time, you will then need to reflect and have a "come-to-Jesus" moment with yourself and your money. Now, if you are already savvy and smart with your money, that is great; I would still ask you to see how you could level up and become even wiser. What little pleasures of life are you indulging in that could be cut, so that you could further invest in either yourself or your business?

Emotional intelligence is a theme in *Entrepreneurship Empowered*, and it is also critical in money management. One component of emotional intelligence is having the ability to say "no" to people, places, and things. You need to become emotionally intelligent when it comes to your money. Learn how to trim the fat. Stop eating out so much. Stop buying coffee every day. Make your own at home. If you wish to be matrix-free, stop feeding the matrix. Knowing how to manage your money is a must. If you don't know how to manage your money, then you surely will not know how to manage a business's money. Poor financial planning and mismanaging of funds are two of the main reasons why businesses fail.

Mindset is everything. Our minds are extremely powerful. It has taken me years upon years to rewire my mind. With regard to money, I am still learning, just like each of you. But I am certainly wiser today than I was in the past. When I first bought my business, I had a poverty mindset. I had been so poor for so long, I really didn't know how to handle the money of the business. I didn't know how to even pay myself. I just picked at the money. I bought STFF in 2002, and it wasn't until 2004 that I bought furniture for my house. I lived in a house with no living room furniture for two years, but all the while I had the money. I can clearly remember Dan (the man I bought my business from) coming to see me for Christmas the first year I owned STFF. I had the biggest Christmas tree in the front room of my house with the most beautifully wrapped gifts underneath, and inside were some of the best gifts one could imagine. There were presents everywhere. I mean, the floor was COVERED. Dan said, "*Natasha, I love your tree, but where is your furniture?*" I kindly replied, "*I finally am able to give quality gifts to those I love.*" He said, "*But what about you?*"

It took me almost fifteen years from that point to finally think about me. Don't lose that much time. How old are you? Now how long have you been subjecting yourself to the weight of others? Gifting everyone else but never gifting yourself? Well, let's stop all that silliness right now and start with this.... **Pay yourself first!**

There is a survival mindset, and there is an abundant mindset. The survival mindset will have you forever stuck in poverty. You will steal, you will sell your body, you will do things that are unspeakable, and you will hate yourself time and time again for living in such a mindset. I lived in a survival mindset for a very long time. Then I met a wonderful woman by the name of Susan Davison. I had the honor of working side by side with her on some awesome projects, and even today, I still work with her. Susan is a financial expert. At one point in her life, she was a stockbroker. She has many stories regarding the New York Stock Exchange and what it was like to work the floor. She is also an energy worker and one of my gurus. She has given me tip after tip regarding the abundant mindset. I said to myself, "*What the hell can I lose by trying some of these tips out?*" It all starts in the mind, remember.

So, I deliberately worked on my thinking and how I spoke. I started by writing once a month about the abundance I wanted. Abundance is not just about money. I would ask for anything—from money to nail growth, to hair growth, to health, to classes, to workshops, to love, and so on. We get so hung up on money, but I demand abundance in all areas of my life.

Suddenly, it was like someone poured the rain of abundance on my head, and I promise, it has yet to shut off. Now I don't request the abundance; I give thanks for it. I am grateful. Gratitude is key. What do you want to see in regard to your finances? Do you need more money? Oh, hell, we all do, so YES is your answer. Then track your money, make the adjustments, live in an abundant mindset, speak life, and be grateful. It really is that simple. But it requires discipline. Next level steps required:

"My revenue was $4 million my first year in business, off of one $20 item."

—Sara Blakely, billionaire businesswoman

Financial Planning

Imagine that: one $20 item generates you $4 million in revenue. Sign me up! **Revenue** is defined in accounting as *"the income that a business has from its normal business activities, usually from the sale of goods and services to customers. Revenue is also referred to as sales or turnover. Some companies receive revenue from interest, royalties, or other fees."* In *Entrepreneurship Empowered*, you must understand the revenue model, which is a framework for how you will generate income for your business. You must have a revenue strategy. You will want to start by asking yourself some questions:

- *How much are my customers willing to pay?*
- *How many customers do I need?*
- *How much revenue can be generated through sales?*

- *If I have more than one revenue stream, how much does each stream contribute to the total?*

The answers to these questions will guide you as you develop your financial plan. Be sure to take your time developing this piece of your business puzzle. It is very important. We will discuss in just a few paragraphs the basics of accounting and the break-even point, which are both very important and must be considered when developing your financial plan.

I would encourage you to research the different types of revenue models. There are several. I am only going to share my top three picks: unit sales, subscription, and freemium. Unit sales measures the amount of revenue generated by the number of items (units) sold by a company. This is the one I used in my business. My revenue was generated by the number of files I sold. The more files I sold, the more money I made. What was so cool was that I could process five to seven files in an hour's time. That is with just one worker. Give me two workers and I doubled that. Give me a scanner and I am now able to process ten to twenty files in an hour's time.

Do the math with me: I charge a base rate of $25 per 100 pages. Then $5 for each additional hundred or a fraction thereof. The average file is about 250 to 300 pages. So, the average file is $35 to $40. This was my rate when I started. My base rate today is double that.

The average work time in my line of business is four hours. In that amount of time, we can execute anywhere between twenty-eight and eighty files. Now multiply that by $40. What number did you get? It is anywhere between $1,100 and $3,200, conservatively, in a four-hour period. It cost me no more than $100 in labor for those four hours. I need everyone to say it with me now…WINNING!

The subscription model is an ever-growing model, and to be honest with you, it is absolutely brilliant. You will see by tracking your money that you are probably signed up in some type of subscription that you are not using. Let's start with that gym membership you have had for twelve years a slave now, and you have only been to once in all those years. A subscription revenue model charges a customer for continual use of the product and or service. The box subscription is hot! We love a box showing up at our door. This is why Amazon is a trillion-dollar company. You can create a subscription for just about anything. So, when thinking about your product or service, how can you use it as a subscription base? With direct payment, of course. The electronic funds transfer is your friend in this model.

"The best things in life are free. The second best are very expensive."

—Coco Chanel, fashion designer

The freemium revenue model is another one of my favorites. Who doesn't love something free? We all do. I used to say for the longest time that I was the queen of free—I mean, I am one resourceful lady. You will see by the time you are done with this book how many resources I have provided to you. How many companies can you name right now that offer some type of freemium? Think about it. There are thousands of them. Cell phone providers are one of the biggest. Right now, I can get a free tablet, but I will pay for the service. Then I will end up paying for extra charges because, of course, the first one or two levels of services will not cover all the usage. Just because something is free doesn't mean we don't pay for it somewhere else. There is a psychology behind pricing. We will cover that in just a bit.

I want you to think about how you could offer some type of freemium with your business. On the space provided, do a little brainstorming and see what you come up with. Also, out of my top three revenue models, which do you think would work best for you? Add what you come up with to your notes, and when you start to develop your financial plan, you can come back to your notes and build from what you came up with.

ENTREPRENEURSHIP EMPOWERED

A New Millennium Business Guide from Start Up to Succession

"Don't ever let your business get ahead of the financial side of your business. Accounting, accounting, accounting. Know your numbers."

—Tilman J. Fertitta, billionaire businessman

Accounting

I often remind my students that it is perfectly fine to hire someone smarter than you, but don't ever not *know your numbers*. I worked for an attorney for a short period of time. He asked me to figure out why he was losing so much money. He owned one firm and worked as a partner in another firm. He was taking money from the firm he was partnered with in order to pay taxes to the firm he owned. Now get this: the firm he owned had a revenue of almost two million dollars. Yes, you read that right. Almost two million dollars.... You are taking money from another firm to pay the taxes. That's a big red flag. I assured him that I would investigate. I said, *"Let me see the last three years of profit and loss statements."* (A profit and loss statement is also known as the *income statement*.) The next thing out his mouth was, *"I don't even know how to read those things."*

Are you kidding me right now?! Don't let this be you. Because he didn't know how to read them, and he trusted his bookkeeper and operations manager, he was getting screwed over. The bookkeeper and operations manager were mother and daughter. They had been ripping him off for years. They were able to get away with hundreds of thousands of dollars. But trust this: whatever is done in the dark will come to light. There is more to this story, and I will share it with you in the leadership and ethics chapter. For now, just take with you this much: **know your numbers!**

There are a few financial reports I want you to become familiar with: the *income statement, balance sheet,* and *cash flow*. They are the three most important reports in *Entrepreneurship Empowered*. The **income statement** is a financial report that measures the financial performance of your business on a monthly or annual basis.

The income statement tells you just that: how much income (profit/loss) you made. As I stated in the previous paragraph, it is also called the profit and loss statement, because it will show both. I want you to always be in the black. Not the red. If you haven't heard the saying *being in the black or red*, let me tell you what it means. The **black means profit**, and the **red means loss.** Some businesses do go into the red. It is common for start-ups to be in the red, but you don't want to stay there. You simply cannot stay there and survive in business. Below is an example of an income statement.

Entrepreneurship Empowered Income Statement Model January 1 through December 31, 20___		
Net Sales	$725,425	
Less: Cost of Goods Sold	456,740	
Gross Income		$268,685
Operating Expenses:		
Salaries	$125,698	
Utilities	8,689	
Depreciation	15,025	
Rent	3,500	
Building Services	5,985	
Insurance	6,200	
Interest	2,585	
Office Supplies	13,259	
Sales Promotion	16,120	
Taxes and Licenses	6,848	
Maintenance	1,258	
Delivery	3,895	
Miscellaneous	1,125	
Total Expenses		$210,187
Net Income Before Taxes		58,498
Less: Income Taxes		14,624
Net Income After Taxes		43,874

I would look at my income statement all the time. More than monthly, but for sure each month after all the numbers were plugged in, I was running a report. The report would show me the revenue generated from the number of files I produced. It would also show me all the expenses I generated. I use Intuit QuickBooks, a very simple software, to record all my business accounting. There is a ton of different training out there if you need help learning it. I recommend QuickBooks, as it is the go-to business accounting software and very user-friendly. However, please keep in mind that you must enter the data correctly because if you don't, the software will spit incorrect data back at you. The balance sheet tells you right off the bat in its name something very important: the report must balance. If it doesn't balance, something is wrong. I never used a balance sheet. It was not that important to me. The profit and loss, however, is what I used all the time. That was the most important accounting report for my business. I do, however, understand the importance of a balance sheet. The **balance sheet** is a financial report that shows what the company owes and what it owns, including shareholders' stake, at a particular point in time. The balance sheet has a particular formula, which, again, must be balanced. This is the fundamental accounting equation: Assets = Liabilities + Owner's Equity. Below is an example of the balance sheet.

Entrepreneurship Empowered Balance Sheet Model December 31, 20___			
Assets			
Current Assets:			
Cash		$ 8,758	
Accounts Receivable		61,984	
Inventory		82,054	
Prepaid Expenses		1,650	
Total Current Assets			$154,446
Fixed Assets:			
Equipment	$100,750		
Building	54,965		
Gross Fixed Assets		$155,715	
Less Accumulated Depreciation		19,985	
Net Fixed Assets			138,730
Total Assets			$293,176
Liabilities and Owners Equity			
Current Liabilities:			
Accounts Payable		$62,482	
Accrued Payable		4,640	
Total Current Liabilities		$67,122	
Long – Term Liabilities:			
Mortgage Payable		32,680	
Total Liabilities			$ 99,802
Owners' Equity:			
Capital Stock		165,000	
Retained Earnings		28,374	
Total Equity			193,374
Total Liabilities and Owners Equity			$293,176

The balance sheet is going to show you the big picture, help you measure the value of your business, and can serve as an early warning system. The balance sheet is also something that current or potential investors will want to look at and interpret. They will want to know how their investment is doing or will do.

I am sure by this point you are wondering what all these different accounting terms mean. After I introduce you to the third and final report, *cash flow*, I will be providing you with some key accounting terms. Because accounting really has its own language, I need you to be familiar with the meanings of those terms. The **cash flow statement** is a financial report that details the inflows and outflows of cash for a company over a set period of time. Below is an example of the cash flow statement.

Entrepreneurship Empowered
Cash Flow Statement Model
For the Year Ended December 31, 20____

Cash Flow From Operations

Net Income..	89,500
Adjustments for depreciation............................	2,500
Adjustments for increased inventories.................	(25,000)
Adjustments for decrease in accounts receivable.......	13,000
Net Cash Flow from Operations..........................	68,300

Cash Flow from Investing

Cash receipts from sale of property and equipment....	12,000
Cash paid for purchase of equipment.....................	(14,000)
Net Cash Flow from Investing............................	(2,000)

Cash Flow from Financing

Cash paid for loan repayment.............................	(6,500)
Net Cash Flow from Financing...........................	(6,500)

Net Increase in Cash	59,800

You always want to be aware of your flow of cash. "*Cash is king.*" I know you have heard that before, right? If not, well, now you have. Here's another good one for you: "*No finance, no romance.*" Oh hell, we better get our money right then! Understanding the flow of cash is super important in business. It will show you if you have enough cash on hand to pay for your current liabilities. Here is where money management really comes into play. You must know how to handle the money in the most effective and efficient way. You must be wise with your business spending habits, just as you need to be wise with your personal spending habits.

The cash flow statement has three components, though not all businesses use all three:

1. *Cash from operating activities*
2. *Cash from investing activities*
3. *Cash from financing activities*

The operating activities is the most commonly used component in small business. It will consider the current expenses, as well as the current accounts receivable. The cash flow statement complements the balance sheet and income statement and is a mandatory part of a company's financial reports since 1987 and still required today in *Entrepreneurship Empowered.*

Terms and definitions as defined by the dictionary:

Revenue: the value received by a firm in return for a good or service.

Expenses: the costs of labor, goods, and services.

Cost of Goods Sold: the total cost in terms of raw materials, labor, and overhead of the business that can be allocated to production.

Net Income: the total revenue in an accounting period minus all expenses during the same period. If income taxes and interest are not deducted, it is called operating profit (or loss, as the case may be).

Assets: the things a business owns. Includes cash, accounts receivable, inventory, equipment, and building.

Current Assets: cash and other assets that are expected to be converted to cash within a year.

Fixed Assets: long-term tangible pieces of property that a firm owns and uses in its operations to generate income. Fixed assets take longer than a year to convert to cash.

Accounts Receivable: current assets resulting from selling a product on credit.

Goodwill (not the store): is a long-term (or noncurrent) asset categorized as an intangible asset.

Intangible Assets: an asset that is not physical in nature. Goodwill, brand recognition, and intellectual property, such as patents, trademarks, and copyrights, are all intangible assets.

Long-Term Investments: is an account on the asset side of a company's balance sheet that represents the company's investments, including stocks, bonds, real estate, and cash that it intends to hold for more than a year.

Liabilities: is defined as a company's legal financial debts or obligations that arise during the course of business operations.

Current Liabilities: are debts payable within one year.

Accounts Payable: money owed by a company to its creditors.

Accrued Expenses: are payments that a company is obligated to pay in the future for which goods and services have already been delivered.

Short-Term Debt: is an account shown in the current liabilities portion of a company's balance sheet. This account is made up of any debt incurred by a company that is due within one year.

Long-Term Debt: consists of loans and financial obligations lasting over one year. Long-term debt for a company would include any financing or leasing obligations that are to come due after a 12-month period.

Shareholder Equity: also referred to as the owner's residual claim after debts have been paid, is equal to a firm's total assets minus its total liabilities.

Retained Earnings: are the profits that a company has earned to date, less any dividends or other distributions paid to investors.

Capital Stock: the number of common and preferred shares that a company is authorized to issue, according to its corporate charter.

Funding and Start-Up Costs

What are the steps to funding your business? For me, I was self-funded. I had enough money generating that I didn't need to take any loans out for STFF. I did, however, borrow money from my uncle for Italian Tans; other than that, my businesses were completely self-funded.

What's super-hot these days is **crowdfunding**. I think many of you have already been exposed to some form of crowdfunding. Crowdfunding is used in many ways, not just business, but it seems to be most successful in business. The word tells you about its meaning: a crowd of people come together to fund your business. Crowdfunding is not a loan. The money you receive doesn't need to be paid back. In some cases, it is like a prepayment for your product or service. In others, it is more an offering of support in exchange for some swag, which could be a T-shirt, a coffee cup, or the like. The Crowdfunding Centre's May 2014 report identified two primary types of crowdfunding:

1. *Rewards crowdfunding: entrepreneurs pre-sell a product or service to launch a business concept without incurring debt or sacrificing equity/shares.*
2. *Equity crowdfunding: the backer receives shares of a company, usually in its early stages, in exchange for the money pledged.*

The SBA has some really awesome tutorials regarding crowdfunding. I highly recommend you take a look at them. One of the colleges I teach at is in Grass Valley, California— a very small town with a lot of charm and character. I bring in one of the local business owners to speak to my students about crowdfunding. She owns a restaurant called Three Forks Bakery & Brewing Co. She was able to raise $45,000 through crowdfunding. Her success with crowdfunding is incredible. She shares her story not only with my students, but with other business professionals in the town, and she has been instrumental in helping and starting crowdfunding campaigns. All of that results in receiving large sums of money.

She will tell you, and so will I, that you must have a really good story. People want to hear your story. They also want to see that you are invested. If you are not invested in your own business, how do you expect someone else to be invested? That sounds silly, but you would be surprised how many people are not invested. They, however, are not Empowered Entrepreneurs. So, tell your story. What's your background? What are your dreams for your business? This will help humanize and frame your case. Share your achievements and progress. What have you invested in your business already?

You are also going to need to have a solid plan. It doesn't need to be some in-depth formal business plan, but it does need to have some key drivers. These include market research, competitive analysis, financials, and expected return.

With crowdfunding, you must be fully committed to the process. You must understand that even though it is a fantastic opportunity for a small business to enter, not all small businesses should do so. And it certainly should not be taken lightly. You will need to make sure you don't miss one call or one email. You will need to make sure you are pitching your business on a daily basis. You will need to make sure you are focused on your target market. You must plan how you are going to create a buzz and keep it going.

It is wise to date your potential customer—and here is where we will roll back the clock a bit. You are not going to date them like we do in the new millennium—fast and in a hurry. You will need to court them for some time and find out what they really like in order to provide the rewards that will entice them to invest. Then, when it's time to launch the crowdfunding, your audience will be excited, and your business will be off to a good start.

There are many different crowdfunding sites in the market today. I would like for you to do a little research on the following top four. Make notes as you research, using the space provided. You should be able to find pros and cons, as well as important information, such as how much of a cut they take from what you raise, and whether there are any additional charges. The research you gather will help you to select which site is best for your business needs. The top four sites are *Kickstarter, GoFundMe, Indiegogo, and Patreon.*

There are other ways to fund your business. I have now given you information on two of four ways: number one, self-funding; number two, crowdfunding. The third and fourth ways are through loans and investors. **Loans** are a lump sum of money you receive, commonly from a bank or other financial institution. You pay back loans with interest. The SBA backs 80% of the small business loans in the United States. They don't lend you the money; remember, they only back you. You must be credit-worthy for any loan. Your business must be in good financial standing and have a solid foundation. Typically for a business loan, you need a traditional business plan, which must include an expense sheet and financial projections for up to five years. We covered business plans in Chapter Four. If you recall, I advised you to pay for someone to write your plan for you. I am once again making that same recommendation: if you are seeking a loan—and a large one at that—please pay for a professional to help you write the plan. You will be more likely to receive the funding you need. Now, if your credit is not right and your business is not in good financial standing, then please don't waste your time. You will not get a loan. It is as simple as that.

There are two types of **investors**: angel investors and venture capitalists. They are both very different. An angel investor is normally a wealthy person who provides funding to a business start-up in exchange for convertible debt or ownership equity. Angel investors are often retired entrepreneurs or executives who may be interested in angel investing for reasons that go beyond pure monetary return. These include wanting to keep abreast of current developments in a particular business arena, mentoring another generation of entrepreneurs, and making use of their experience and networks on a less-than-full-time basis. Thus, in addition to funds, angel investors can often provide valuable management advice and important contacts.

Venture capitalists, on the other hand, provide funding after an initial seed funding has already been given. Seed funding could come from crowdfunding or an angel investor.

Venture capitalists commonly take on high-risk companies for a high return. A venture capitalist is a person who makes venture investments, and these venture capitalists are expected to bring managerial and technical expertise, as well as capital, to their investments. A venture capital fund refers to a pooled investment vehicle (in the United States, often an LP or LLC) that primarily invests the financial capital of third-party investors in enterprises that are too risky for the standard capital markets or bank loans. These funds are typically managed by a venture capital firm, which often employs individuals with technology backgrounds (scientists, researchers), business training, and/or deep industry experience.

Before you even begin to look for funding, you will need to know what your start-up costs are going to be. Keep in mind there is no cookie-cutter recipe for businesses. Each one is going to have different needs and expenses. There is no one-size-fits-all financial solution. You are going to need to make a start-up expenses worksheet. There are several different templates available that you can download and type directly into. The following are typical start-up costs that you are likely to face—regardless of your business type:

- Office space
- Equipment and supplies
- Communications
- Utilities
- Licenses and permits
- Insurance
- Inventory
- Employee salaries
- Advertising and marketing
- Market research
- Printed marketing material
- Making a website
- Lawyers and accountants

Don't underestimate your start-up costs. Do your research. I would even encourage you to add 5–10% to each of your start-up costs. I would rather you have excess than be short. When doing your research for start-up costs, it is wise to reach out to someone who is in a similar field of business and ask them what costs they have incurred. Normally, others in business are open to speaking with aspiring entrepreneurs. If someone says no, then just keep searching until you find someone. There's plenty of information right at your fingertips. That is where you start. Remember, you are an Empowered Entrepreneur!

ENTREPRENEURSHIP EMPOWERED

Chapter 7: Leadership and Ethics

"The function of leadership is to produce more leaders, not more followers."

—Ralph Nader, political activist

The topics we are now going to dive into are some of my very favorites. Each of them I hold dearly. Everything ultimately stems from them in *Entrepreneurship Empowered*. I love the quote that I started this chapter with because, well, I truly believe that is what makes a great leader. Not that I have more followers, but rather that I am able to build up more leaders. Many of the employees I have had have gone on to hold leadership roles. Several of them have become business owners themselves. Today, many of my students become leaders, and, most importantly, they become stronger at leading their own lives. To me, this is one of the greatest gifts I am able to give them.

I want you to think for a moment about some great leaders. They can be anyone from celebrities to bosses to family, even fictional characters. Think about what made them such great leaders. If they are personal leaders to you, what was it you really admired about them? Why did you see them as such great leaders? Then I want you to think about what types of behaviors they had. What type of spirit did they carry? Then, for a moment, I want you to think about the concept of being a born leader versus being able to build a leader. In the space provided, write what comes to you.

_____

_____

_____

_____

_____

_____

_____

_____

_____

_____

_____

_____

_____

_____

_____

_____

_____

_____

_____

_____

_____

_____

_____

_____

A New Millennium Business Guide from Start Up to Succession

Are leaders made, or are they born? I swear I came out of the womb saying, *"Charge, forward we go!"* For the longest time, I really felt like I was a natural-born leader and that all great leaders must have been born that way. Many of you may feel the same way. However, I will tell you that leaders can be made. As I stated above, I believe that true leaders build up more leaders. I also firmly believe that a boss will tell you what to do, but a leader will show you. A leader will get on the ground with you. I promise you that I am working right alongside you. I am leading by example.

As I have grown in my leadership ability, I have learned that leadership, like so many other things in life, is an inside job. That means you must be able to lead yourself. Are there leaders out there who are not right within? Absolutely. But in my humble opinion, I believe they will never reach the highest vibrational leadership level unless they are able to be right within. I know this doesn't seem true, especially in the world we live in (aka "the jungle"). But I can attest from my own experience that I was a great leader, but once I got my shit together and started healing within, I became a ridiculously amazing leader—my highest vibrational leadership level yet. I am building up more leaders now than ever before. I am also serving more of the masses than ever before. My territory has expanded, and my leadership role has increased. Some of you are great leaders, but I need you to become ridiculously amazing leaders. I cannot, nor do I wish, to be out in these streets alone. I need you to understand that *the way out is within*. It is your job to help free yourself so that you may serve others and provide them with the tools they need to be free. Remember, freedom comes in pieces—this is yet another piece given to you today.

Leaders commonly have a core set of qualities. Though each leader is different in their own right, there does tend to be a theme with many of the greatest leaders of all time. *Honesty and integrity* are often right at the top of the list of qualities. These qualities will tie directly in with ethics, which we will cover in just a few paragraphs. People can smell fakeness, and far too often, liars are only really lying to themselves. Eventually, the truth comes out, one way or another. In *Entrepreneurship Empowered*, leaders must be honest and have integrity. If not, they will create a culture that is dishonest—a business that is dishonest. You can look at the Enron case and see that corrupt leadership only leads to corrupt business. If you haven't heard about the Enron case, I recommend you examine it. That will hold space for a very long time as an example of what not to do in business. It is one of the most highly discussed and studied ethics cases in the United States and around the world.

Confidence is critical to leadership. Especially because leadership is about inspiring others. In order to truly inspire, you must be confident in what you are offering to others. You must be able to have confidence in your people that they will do right by you. That they will take what you are giving them, and they will run with it. Again, true leaders are building up other leaders, not followers.

Please don't confuse arrogance with confidence. Arrogant leaders are often single-minded. They believe they are superior. They may be highly intelligent, but they are usually socially inept. You know someone like that, don't you? Confident leaders don't need to offend others. They see the potential in others and have a desire to help them succeed. Confident leaders will rarely tell you how wrong you are. They will give you advice and wisdom on how to be a better person. They will never put you down for being human. Arrogant leaders, however, will ridicule you and often belittle you, even in front of your peers. So much bullying goes on in the workplace, and as a result, the employee turnover rate is extremely high. So is poor performance.

Communication is very different in an arrogant leader than in a confident leader. An arrogant leader is always trying to one-up almost everything that is said and done. A confident leader is not going to impose his or her vision on you, but rather inspire you by showing how powerful and accomplished one is, or can be, by fulfilling the vision. Being an effective communicator is mandatory for

Entrepreneurship Empowered. Effective communication not only comes from speaking, but also listening and observation. All great leaders will take the time to listen to those under their command. They will also observe, in order to hear what isn't spoken. Then they will take all of what they have learned and use it when they communicate their message.

Words are extremely powerful. Another main reason why I am now a ridiculously amazing leader, in addition to getting my shit together and healing within, is because I understand the power of words. I speak life and I use my words to *EMPOWER* and uplift those I serve and lead. I encourage others to do the same. Words are very powerful. "*I am...*" is by far the most powerful statement of all, because what you put after, you will ultimately be. Two other little words that are very powerful: THANK YOU! I cannot tell you how often those two words are underused. You, I am sure, have done many things in your life and have not received a thank you. Well, guess what? Right now, I say THANK YOU! For what it's worth, this world will be disrespectful time and time again. I encourage you not to be disrespectful. If you are a leader, you had better know how to be respectful and have gratitude or you will stay below par and your vibrational level will eventually be no more.

Humility is a key core competency of a leader. I have more power on the ground in a place of humility than I do standing above you, screaming and waving my hands around like a crazy lady—which I can do, mind you, because I am an Italian who gets loud and talks with her hands. But now I use that energy to tell jokes and entertain. With leadership, I am much more humble. Being humble and using emotional intelligence allows me to hold space for others, make sound decisions, and be more creative. All of which are very important to leadership. A good study to look at is that of Ou, Waldman, and Peterson. It was published in the *Journal of Management* in 2015, and the article is entitled "Do Humble CEOs Matter?" This study of 105 IT companies found that greater humility in their CEOs was associated with greater leadership team integration, greater collaboration and cooperation, and greater flexibility in strategic orientation.[19]

Humble leaders are working toward the good of others and society, not themselves. Humble leaders stay hungry. They never stop learning, they are authentic in every way, they give up being right, and they give way to asking the right questions. They have a servant's heart and understand the true power of service.

Emotional intelligence is something you have seen me address several times before. Here it is, yes, again. I promise you, the more emotionally intelligent you become, the freer you are, the more powerful you become, and the more impact you have. *Entrepreneurship Empowered* demands you to be emotionally intelligent. Brilliance takes many forms— emotional intelligence is certainly one form. It allows you to have acute awareness with regard to your own emotions and those whom you serve. That acute awareness is crucial for sound decision-making, which we all know is required in leadership. With regard to others, you can create strategies that keep them grounded as you deliver either good or bad news. Mental health is an epidemic in our world. The jungle is filled with the craziest animals you have ever seen. You are one of them. (Don't look at my words like that, you know I am telling the truth. You get hangry, too!)

Emotionally intelligent leaders tend to have a better grasp on mental health and are able to assess the mental state of their employees. They know if someone is suffering from depression, anxiety, grief, trauma, and the like. They are then able to serve them by providing the resources they need. Being supportive has a direct effect on the productivity of the business. The healthier the employees, the healthier the company. Emotionally intelligent leaders understand the importance of humor. Laughter is medicine for the soul, they say, and I would have to agree. I am confident you have laughed at me several times while reading this book. I promise you that I am much funnier in person. You can connect with me in person or even virtually, and I will work one-on-one with you regarding your business needs. My services come with a fee, of course, but my jokes are free.

"You can't relate to a superhero, to a superman, but you can identify with a real man who in times of crisis draws forth some extraordinary quality from within himself and triumphs but only after a struggle."

—Timothy Dalton, British actor

I remember it like it was yesterday. Dan Acland, the man I worked for and bought my business from, told me something I have never forgotten and that I share with my students and clients all the time: *"When the plane is crashing, DO NOT PANIC. Get up from the pilot's seat, walk calmly to the back of the plane, fix the plane, calmly walk to the front of the plane, have a seat in the pilot's seat, and continue to fly the plane."* A leader is not a leader if they are not able to handle crisis. You will not convince me otherwise. In *Entrepreneurship Empowered*, you must be able to handle crises. They are going to happen time and time again. I started this chapter by telling you how important it is to be right within to be a highly effective, ridiculously amazing leader. The power within you is what will help you in times of crisis. You will draw on that strength and you will lead your team and all those around you to safety. The following excerpt comes from an article in *Forbes*, entitled "How Training Like A Pilot Will Set You Up For Success In Crisis Management," by Robert Glazer. *"Pilots engage in some of the most rigorous training of any profession. They constantly prepare for disastrous situations and practice maneuvers that are unlikely to occur, such as landing a plane with one engine. While most of us will never face these situations, there is a core principle that pilots are taught for handling emergencies that we could all learn from: the ANC protocol. The ANC protocol stands for Aviate, Navigate and Communicate, in that order.*

- *Aviate – Maintain control of the aircraft*

- *Navigate – Know where you are and where you intend to go*
- *Communicate – Let someone know your plans and needs*"[20]

Communication comes after gaining control and figuring out what needs to be done. This takes place inside the mind and heart of a leader. Communication is not needed any time before that. It will only cause panic. Just imagine, if you will, staying with the plane example, how much panic and chaos would erupt if a pilot jumped right to communicating issues to the passengers on board. The energy alone would bring down the plane. We underestimate energy so much. It is critical for the pilot to take control, navigate, and then release information as needed. I highly recommend you research crisis tactics, and even examine the military. They deal with crisis situations all the time. The better equipped you are to handle crises, the more successful you will be in life and in business. Whatever you do, DO NOT PANIC.

There is great power in remaining calm. I want you to remember this, not just in business, but also in your daily life. You are the leader of your life. Make sure to stay calm when emotions run high. I need you to fully activate your emotional intelligence and use every drop of it. When crises arise—and they will time and time again—I need you to take control of them. I need you to look at them with a clear mind. Being sober-minded is very important. Calm is your superpower. Let's take a closer look at that. The following are definitions from the dictionary:

- **Calm** is having the absence of strong emotions
- **Super** refers to an extraordinary ability
- **Power** is the capacity and size of your influence

So how do you truly stay calm under pressure? It starts with your overall character. It starts with your thought process. There is great power in positive thinking. Most great leaders who operate out of a calm demeanor have an incredible mind. They are very positive in thought and in nature. American philosopher and psychologist William James once said, "*The greatest weapon against stress is our ability to choose one thought over another.*" When stressful thoughts come into your mind, you must release them. You must not give way to them because they are cancerous and will multiply like gremlins. You need to avoid them, just like you need to avoid negative people. They, too, can cause you great stress. Energy is real. It is important as a leader to be careful with your energy—what you give off and what you receive—especially during a time of crisis.

Another skill a calm leader has is that they understand how important it is to only focus on one thing at a time. Multitasking is an illusion, and though many people believe they are a master of it, they are only delaying themselves from truly being effective and efficient. They are really training themselves to be distracted. The brain can only think of one thing at a time. Multitasking often makes you speed up, but what you really need to do is slow down. When you slow down, you can be more engaged in the task at hand and churn out better work. The same goes for problem-solving. When you slow down and break the problem into smaller pieces, you can solve the issue. Leadership is an art. It seems to be dying in our world. Therefore, I need you to rise up and remember that you are an Empowered Entrepreneur. You are going to be the catalyst that brings life back to leadership. But it all starts with you. You must start now to train your mind to be calm. You must remember that it is one of your superpowers.

There are two leadership theories I not only teach but practice myself. *Situational leadership* is one, and *transformation leadership* is the other. **Situational leadership** has its origin from the early 1970s but still holds value today in the new millennium. It was developed by Ken Blanchard and Paul Hersey. It is a practical guide to almost any workplace situation. Can you guess the main theme behind situational leadership? The name really says it. It is based on the situation at hand. The best leadership style to use is dependent on the situation. It is also dependent on the maturity and skill level of the followers. This changes from situation to situation and from person to person.

The Four Leadership Styles

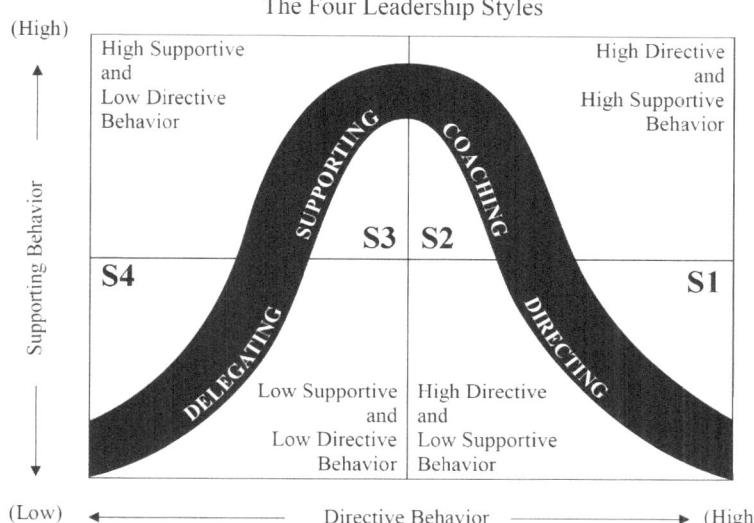

Follower Maturity	Leadership Style	Leadership Behavior	Guidance
Followers are unable to do the task and insecure.	S1 Directing	High Task & Low Relationship	Define the roles and task for each follower and then supervise them closely. Important decisions are to be made by the leader and announced to the followers.
Followers are unable to take responsibility but are willing to take on the task.	S2 Coaching	High Task & High Relationship	Define the roles and tasks of each follower, but also seek ideas and suggestions from followers. The leader coaches the followers as they develop their skills and abilities.
Followers are experienced and able to do the task but are unwilling to take on the responsibility.	S3 Supporting	Low Task & High Relationship	The leader shares decision making with the followers. A participating leader will facilitate discussions and lead the followers toward increased control over the work.
Followers are experienced in the task and confident in the ability.	S4 Delegating	Low Task & Low Relationship	While still involved in the decision, the delegating leader allows the followers to "run their own show". In fact the followers will decide when to get leader involve.

Both charts were created by Entrepreneurship Empowered based on the Situational Leadership Model by Blanchard and Hersey

There are four different leadership styles within situational leadership: style one is **directing**, style two is **coaching**, style three is **supporting**, and style four is **delegating**. View the charts to better understand. If you attend one of my classes, I will go into more detail regarding situational leadership. But for now, I would like for you to take some time to review the information on the charts and try the activity that follows.

Below is a set of situations. You are going to choose what to do, and what you choose to do will indicate what type of leadership style you used. Use the charts to help you.

Situational Leadership Styles Activity

1. You are the project manager of a six-man team. You encourage your team and notice that they work well together. However, a conflict arises between two team members regarding which idea to use in the next stage of the project. As their leader, you:

What is your leadership style?

2. You are the new head basketball coach. You notice that morale is low, the players are not performing at the level you know they are capable of, and they lack new skill techniques that you know will help them be more successful in the game. In a meeting, you:

What is your leadership style?

3. You hire a new employee who has a strong administrative skill set. After only a few weeks with the new employee, you can tell she is innovative and communicates well with clients. At first, you:

What is your leadership style?

4. You ask one of your long-time employees to take on a new task. His past performance shows that he has done well with your direction and support. The new task is important in making sure the project is completed on time. He may not have all the skills needed to do the task, but he is enthusiastic about the new challenge. You:

What is your leadership style?

5. Your organization has recently seen an increase in work. You have asked one of your employees to take on a new responsibility. You have worked with him for several years now, and you know that he has the knowledge and skills to be successful. However, he seems insecure about his ability to do the job. You decide to:

What is your leadership style?

6. You are the dean in the business department of a college that is doing well. Student success is important to you. You would like student retention to increase, and you would also like to increase graduation rates. You decide to:

What is your leadership style?

"It takes 20 years to build a reputation and only five minutes to ruin it. If you think about that, you will do things differently."

—Warren Buffett, billionaire investor

Warren Buffett is the business. Just as I have been a leader since I came out of the womb, so, too, has Warren Buffett. Did you know that he reads like five to six hours a day, according to some reports? Do you know what he is reading? Do you know why he reads so much? He is reading newspapers and corporate reports. His net worth is 77.7

BILLION DOLLARS. Hello, somebody. Buffett's leadership style is transformational. He has over 300,000 employees that he inspires, and whose lives are transformed by being under his leadership.

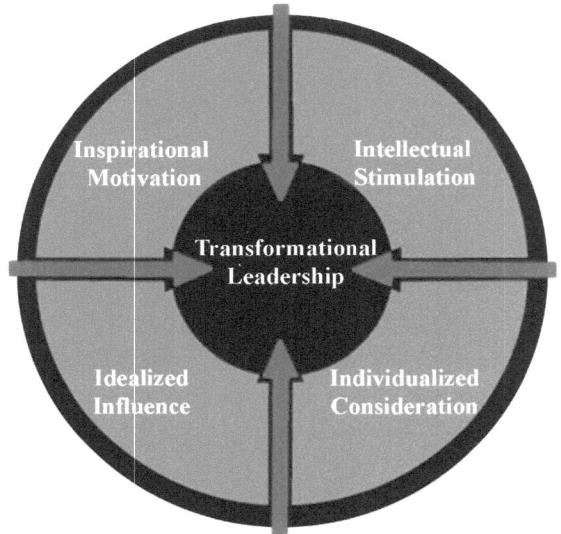

Created by Entrepreneurship Empowered based on
Transformational Leadership Theory; Downton and Burns

What exactly is **transformational leadership**, you ask? According to STU Online, "*Transformational leadership inspires people to achieve unexpected or remarkable results. It gives workers autonomy over specific jobs, as well as the authority to make decisions once they have been trained.*

Some of the basic characteristics of transformational leadership are inspirational, in that the leader can inspire workers to find better ways of achieving a goal; mobilization, because leadership can mobilize people into groups that can get work done, and morale, in that transformational leaders raise the well-being and motivation level of a group through excellent rapport. They are also good at conflict resolution."[21]

Just like situational leadership, transformational leadership originated in the 1970s and is still very relevant today. Buffet will quickly tell you that success doesn't have an age, which is why in almost all of his readings, you will find financial reports from 1967. Even though we are in the new millennium, we can still do and learn a lot by what has taken place in the past. The trick is to use that information wisely so that we excel and make an impact in the future.

According to STU Online, *"transformational leaders specialize in:*

- *Working to change the system*
- *Solving challenges by finding experiences that show that old patterns do not fit or work*
- *Wanting to know what has to change*
- *Maximizing their teams' capability and capacity"*[21]

"Ethics or simple honesty are the building blocks upon which our whole society is based, and business is a part of our society, and it's integral to the practice of being able to conduct business, that you have a set of honest standards."

—Kerry Stokes, billionaire businessman

"Business ethics" often seems to be an oxymoron, right? But just as being a humble leader is critical to being a new millennium leader, so too is being ethical. For a moment, I want you to list all the things that come to mind when you think of ethics, both personally and in business. Use the space provided.

Ethics can often be a gray area. It deals with what is wrong and what is right. But who is to say what that is? Business ethics is different than personal ethics, but they do somewhat overlap. According to the Corporate Finance Institute (CFI), *"Business ethics are the moral principles that act as guidelines for the way a business conducts itself and its transactions. In many ways, the same guidelines that individuals use to conduct themselves in an acceptable way—in personal and professional settings—apply to businesses as well."*[22]

I have not always been a very ethical person. The main reason is that I was once living in a survival mindset. I come from a deep history of poverty, and damn it, my baby needed diapers! I had friends who would steal from the store and then return the merchandise. I could not steal to save my life. I tried it one time and they said, *"Natasha, you had one job, damn it, and you couldn't do it."* I said, *"Give me a different job, then!"* That is just what they did. I no longer was the thief but the professional returner. I would return all kinds of things at several different stores and we would split the money. This was not the only unethical behavior I had. I worked for a restaurant (which will go unnamed), and the manager would say, *"If the customer gives you cash, we will just split the cash and not enter the sale."* I thought, *Well, if the manager is in on it, then it's got to be okay.* We ran with that for some time and my baby had diapers and some clothes. But I continued to stay poor. I never came up out of poverty until I changed my mindset to an abundant one.

I truly believe that now I am an ethical person with a strong moral compass. I choose to do the right thing because I know that it is the best way to live my life. In the last chapter, I told you about an attorney I worked for who didn't know how to read his profit and loss statements. I discovered that not only was there forgery happening, but also embezzlement. I lost my job over finding the information and the attorney let it happen, even though he retained me to find out what was happening to his money.

The reason he let it happen was because he was having an affair with the operations manager. She showed up one early evening to his house highly intoxicated, and his wife answered the door. She demanded to speak with him, and when he came to the door, he said, *"Why are you here?"* She explained that she was getting rid of me and if he dared try to keep me, she would be having a word with his wife. This happened on the same Sunday when I received my email that I was no longer needed. Mind you, I reached out to him and asked what was going on. He said, *"Don't worry, it will be normal business on Monday. You are fine."* I sent that response back to the operations manager in her email to me, and she later responded that my services were no longer needed.

Do you see how that unfolded? She fired me via email, and I contacted him. He told me "normal business on Monday." I responded to her with what he said, and she went to his house and made the threat, then returned the email to me that the services were no longer needed. When I sent him back communication that indeed I was fired, he never responded again. The next time we spoke was in the hearing office, where he offered me a large sum of money. I explained to him that I would not take the money because I could not do to him what they had done to me. I would, however, sue him for wrongful termination because he had insurance that would handle the matter. That is just what I did, and I won.

This case was a hard hit for me, but today I can see it was one of my most powerful personal ethics cases. I use it in all of my classes and share it with my clients as well. I encourage all of them first and foremost: **know your numbers**. Don't you dare not know what is going on with your numbers. But my second plea: **please do the right thing**. Be ethical. The outcome of that company is that it failed. The operations manager and the bookkeeper did get away with hundreds of thousands of dollars, but then it all came to an end. If they would have been ethical, not only would they have made over $1.5 million, but the company would have been so much more profitable. Unethical behavior has a damaging effect on a business and its stakeholders. Leaders must be ethical, and they must strive to hire and retain ethical management and employees.

In *Entrepreneurship Empowered*, you must be ethical. It will affect your bottom line. I want you to understand that you will come across businesses and people who will continually be unethical, and it will seem like they are getting further, or away with a lot. I can promise you that it will come to a head and then their game will be over. Going back to the Enron case, you can clearly see how much they were able to get away with, and it appeared they were living the life. In many respects, they were...then it all came crashing down, and one of the top CEOs blew his brains out in his car in the middle of a park. Game over—just like that. It is not worth it. Don't play the short game. Play the long game.

Leadership is a mastery. It takes time to become a great leader. It takes a great deal of self-awareness. The more self-aware you are, the higher your emotional intelligence and the greater success you will have as a leader. I mentioned it earlier: leadership is dying. Why is it dying? Because we are leading by what we don't know more often than leading by what we do know. The wisdom of one cannot support the minds of many. It is only when each of us is able to use our gifts that we are able to be amazingly powerful. This is the challenge of a new millennium leader. They must understand what dots connect the physical and the energetic realm. They must be able to use the power of humanity as a driving force. This is most often done in a place of humility. This is done in a place of calmness. This is done in a place of deep thought and strategic placement of each person—so that their skills and talents are fully activated.

I am a powerful leader, but I can promise you this much: it is my people who possess the greatest power of all. "*We the people*"—one of the most powerful statements in the United States. But also, one of the most underused resources. We must empty ourselves out and give way to our greatness. We must remove all forms of toxic thought and relationships in order to keep ourselves in tune with our highest frequency. It was that frequency that caused Ali to be the greatest boxer of all time. It's that frequency that will allow you to be the greatest version of yourself. You are an Empowered Entrepreneur, and this is *Entrepreneurship Empowered*.

 **Chapter 8**: Human Resources

"We must lay hold of the fact that economic laws are not made by nature. They are made by human beings."

—Franklin Roosevelt, former U.S. president

We are in the human economy. The human has been the driving force behind all innovation, and really all the other economies we have had prior. In this new millennium, some would say we are at the height of the human economy. I, however, believe that we will continue to rise. We have a love/hate relationship with the human, yet without us, there is no life itself...or is there? That question remains unanswered. To be an Empowered Entrepreneur, you will not only need to understand how to deal with the human, but you will need the human to build your business.

Human relations, also known as HR, is an integral part of an organization. Many businesses have dedicated HR departments to handle all HR needs. Why is that? Because there really is so much to handle, especially when you start to employ more and more people. I personally never had an HR department. I did all the HR myself. However, I never had a large staff. At my height, I had about seventeen part-time employees. I did have an accountant dedicated to just the employee side of the house. I would send over the hours my employees worked, and she would do all the math for me. She would also keep me up with my taxes, which can be very complex and time-consuming. Other than that, I handled everything else.

What is everything else? Each business will differ, but there will be a common theme with all businesses. There will always be a recruiting and selection process. You will need to create job descriptions prior to posting job announcements. The job description should be detailed so that when a new hire does come in, they are able to know what will be required of them. It is important to include certain elements in your job posting that are mission-critical to the job. These include things like being able to lift fifty pounds—if lifting is involved. If you need someone to type at a particular speed or know a particular software, you need to include that in your job announcement. This should help dissuade those who don't possess what you are looking for from applying, but don't be surprised if they do show up in your string of submitted résumés, because they will.

You will get a string of résumés submitted. Many times, employers will get hundreds of résumés a day. Depending on the economy, that is, but overall, people are always looking for work. Finding good help is very hard, however. You will go through all the résumés submitted and narrow them down by those who fit the job description. Then you will need to be very wise with the pool of candidates you have selected to review a little deeper.

In this day and age, the way social media is set up, you can find a virtual footprint of almost anyone. I worked for a firm where one of my job duties was to help with the hiring process. I wrote the job descriptions and job announcements. I then did the pre-selection of candidates and recommended a set of potential applicants to my executives. I can clearly remember one executive saying, *"Let's look at their Facebook."* She went right to googling the person's name and boom, there was the person. To be honest, she just looked at them and judged from their pictures and said, *"No, not that one."*

You will need to remember this when you are applying for jobs yourself. You can easily deactivate your account without completely closing it. You should do this when applying for jobs. Better yet, keep your social media clean. In *Entrepreneurship Empowered*, you will use social media to build your brand awareness, and it should always be respectable. As an employer, there is nothing wrong with viewing profiles, but I do not recommend you make your decisions based on someone's Facebook or any other social media.

After you have selected your three to five potential candidates, you will then move into the interview process. It is good practice to have a set of standard interview questions. This makes the interviewing process fair for all candidates. Your questions should include things that pertain to the job in which the candidate is being interviewed. You will also want to have questions that deal with conflict resolution. Behavior questions are critical, too—they will tell you if the person will fit in with your work culture. Not everyone is fitted for your culture, and that is important to understand.

In the new millennium business world, there is a rise in ethical dilemma questions being asked in interviews. They are just as important, if not more important, than all other questions. You certainly want an ethical person working for you. Time and time again, we see that businesses with ethically strong executives and staff do far better than those who are unethical. Companies that are unethical do not last. Maybe they last for twenty years, but you are in the long game, not the short game—and twenty years is a very short game. So, choose to be ethical and hire ethical people.

Below is a set of standard interview questions. All of the questions come directly from the career sections of

Monster.com. I have used many of these questions myself when interviewing potential employees.

- *"Tell me about yourself.*
- *What are your strengths?*
- *What are your weaknesses?*
- *Why do you want this job?*
- *Where would you like to be in your career five years from now?*
- *What's your ideal company?*
- *What attracted you to this company?*
- *Why should we hire you?*
- *What did you like least about your last job?*
- *When were you most satisfied in your job?*
- *What can you do for us that other candidates can't?*
- *What were the responsibilities of your last position?*
- *Why are you leaving your present job?*
- *What do you know about this industry?*
- *What do you know about our company?*
- *Are you willing to relocate?*
- *Do you have any questions for me?"*

Here are some commonly used behavior questions:
- *"What was the last project you led, and what was its outcome?*
- *Give me an example of a time that you felt you went above and beyond the call of duty at work.*
- *Can you describe a time when your work was criticized?*
- *Have you ever been on a team where someone was not pulling their own weight? How did you handle it?*
- *Tell me about a time when you had to give someone difficult feedback. How did you handle it?*
- *What is your greatest failure, and what did you learn from it?*
- *How do you handle working with people who annoy you?*

- If I were your supervisor and asked you to do something that you disagreed with, what would you do?
- What was the most difficult period in your life, and how did you deal with it?
- Give me an example of a time you did something wrong. How did you handle it?
- Tell me about a time where you had to deal with conflict on the job.
- If you were at a business lunch and you ordered a rare steak and they brought it to you well done, what would you do?
- If you found out your company was doing something against the law, like fraud, what would you do?
- What assignment was too difficult for you, and how did you resolve the issue?
- What's the most difficult decision you've made in the last two years, and how did you come to that decision?
- Describe how you would handle a situation if you were required to finish multiple tasks by the end of the day, and why there was no conceivable way that you could finish them."

In small business, we commonly only have one interview, but you may choose to interview someone two or even three times, depending on the size of your organization and the management structure. You may also have some type of testing required when interviewing. Some companies have you take a simulated online test that shows them information related to the position at hand. There are other tests you may require candidates to take, such as personality tests or basic skills tests.

You will use all the information from the tests and the interview to make your final selection. You will then move into calling and checking references. It is also good practice to have some standard questions ready to ask when checking references. Here are some for you to choose from:

- *"When did (name) work for your company? Could you confirm starting and ending employment dates? When did he/she leave the company?*
- *What was her/his position? Can you describe the job responsibilities?*
- *Could I briefly review (name's) résumé? Does the job title and job description match the position that (name) held?*
- *Why did (name) leave the company?*
- *What was her/his starting and ending salary? (In some locations, employers are precluded from asking about salary due to state and local legislation.)*
- *Did (name) miss a lot of work? Was s/he frequently late? Were there any issues you are aware of that impacted her/his job performance?*
- *Did he/she get along well with management and coworkers?*
- *Can you describe this person's experience working as a member of a team?*
- *Did (name) prefer to work on a team or independently?*
- *How did he/she support coworkers?*
- *What were (name's) strengths and weaknesses as an employee?*
- *Was (name) promoted while with your company?*
- *Did (name) supervise other employees? How effectively? If I spoke to those employees, how do you think they would describe (name's) management style?*
- *How did (name) handle conflict? How about pressure? Stress?*
- *Did you evaluate (name's) performance? Can you speak to her/his strong and weak points? What was noted as needing improvement during their performance review?*
- *What was (name's) biggest accomplishment while working for your company?*
- *Would you rehire (name) if the opportunity arose?*

- *If I describe the position we are hiring for to you, could you describe how good a fit you think (name) would be for the position?*
- *Is there anything I haven't asked that you would like to share with me?"*

The next step of the hiring process is making the offer of employment. You will commonly call the new hire and let them know you would like to offer them the position, and then you will give them a start date. Next is orientation and onboarding. There will always be new hire paperwork that needs to be processed. The paperwork will consist of government-required forms such as the I-9 and W-4. You can go directly to IRS.gov[23] and pull the forms you need. They have a forms section, and the IRS website is fairly user-friendly. The forms are where a person will indicate the number of deductions they will be claiming, which guides how much taxes will be taken from one's income.

A job application or résumé will be included in an employee's file and is often seen as part of the paperwork process. For my business, I had an ethics disclosure agreement that my employees would sign because of the nature of my business. In the new millennium business world, we are seeing a rise in codes of ethics or ethical disclosures in new-hire paperwork processes. Perhaps some of you remember signing something of the same nature. My employees would also sign a non-competition agreement. It clearly stated that if they were to leave my company, they would not go into the market and compete against me. If they did, I would move forward with ligation. I had a company handbook that they also signed. The handbook had information specific to my company and the job role, expectations, and performance outcomes.

Some of the information I didn't have, but most employees will have, is benefit information. My employees were part-time, so I didn't provide benefits. If you have more than fifty full-time employees, you must, by law, provide health insurance coverage at an affordable rate. This information comes directly from the Affordable Health Care

Act. It is very important that, as an employer, you take time to read in detail all that the Affordable Health Care Act states. You can find information on SBA's website. The new hire paperwork is where an employee will select the coverage they would like, and the benefit will be set in place. Once a benefit is set in place, it often cannot be changed again until an open enrollment period comes around. It is wise to make sure your employee understands what they are selecting and what will not be able to be changed for a period.

I could really dive deep into insurance and express how much of a scam it is, but we must move forward. I just wanted to tell you to be wise in what you select for your people as health care options. Please look for the best rates for them. Again, review all the health care options and read over several times the information provided by the Affordable Health Care Act. To ensure your employees understand what they are getting themselves into, please leave nothing out. Make sure they have all the information they need to make the best decision.

Another important piece of the new hire process is clearly laying out how compensation works, and how and when they will be paid. In this new millennium, we hardly write a check anymore. It is rare. Most payments are now done by direct deposit. Most of you can attest to that yourselves—I am sure most of you have direct deposit right now. It has just made things so much simpler. Technology!

When making direct deposits, you will not only need to have employees fill out a form, but you will need their banking information as well. The form they fill out will allow you to have access to their account for the sole purpose of depositing funds. A lot of employers will also give employees a schedule showing exactly when payday occurs. This helps employees manage their money and the bills they have to pay. As a professor, I only get paid once a month, and payday normally falls on the tenth of each month. Well, I need to ensure that all of which is required for me to pay either falls on the tenth or a few days after. That is when the bulk of my money hits. However, I am not only a professor, but also an actively working Empowered Entrepreneur, so I have money streams coming in pretty much always. Even so, I have a contracted guarantee of money that hits my bank the tenth of each month. Because of this, I base a lot of my budgeting around that date.

It is very important to check with your local labor regulations board to ensure you do all that is legally required when hiring employees. After you have collected all the required documents and retained all signed forms, you will need to make sure your employee has copies of everything they have signed. That is very important; they are to receive copies of everything. You will be required to file your forms and keep them on record. They must be safeguarded and protected—always. You now have people's private information. Lock your filing cabinets and, if stored electronically, their employee information must be kept in an encrypted form. Identity theft is big, and it happens—not only to the consumers' data, but employees oftentimes fall victim, too. You must uphold the oath to protect your people and their identities.

Below you will find additional bullet points of all that I have covered so far, and a little more. The following information comes directly from Workable, a recruiting software company. They help you find, track, and hire employees.

- *"An employment contract should include:*
  - *Job information (job title, department)*
  - *Work schedule*
  - *Length of employment*
  - *Compensation and benefits*
  - *Employee responsibilities*
  - *Termination conditions*
- *Most common types of employment forms to complete are:*
  - *W-4 form (or W-9 for contractors)*
  - *I-9 Employment Eligibility Verification form*
  - *State Tax Withholding form*

- o *Direct Deposit form*
- o *E-Verify system: This is not a form, but a way to verify employee eligibility in the U.S.*
- *Possible internal forms.*
  - o *Non-compete agreements*
  - o *Non-disclosure agreements*
  - o *Employee invention forms*
  - o *Employee handbook acknowledgement forms*
  - o *Drug and/or alcohol test consent agreements*
  - o *Job analysis forms (responsibilities, goals and performance evaluation criteria)*
  - o *Employee equipment inventory lists*
  - o *Confidentiality and security agreements*
- *Most common employee benefits are:*
  - o *Life and health insurance*
  - o *Mobile plan*
  - o *Company car*
  - o *Stock options*
  - o *Retirement plan*
  - o *Disability insurance*
  - o *Paid time off/vacation policies (including any paid holidays)*
  - o *Sick leave*
  - o *Employee wellness perks (e.g., gym memberships)*
  - o *Tuition reimbursement*
- *Obtain employees' personal data for emergencies*
  - o *Emergency contacts*
  - o *Brief medical history*
  - o *Food allergies or preferences (e.g., vegan or gluten-free)"*[24]

"Tell me and I forget, teach me and I may remember, involve me and I learn."

—Benjamin Franklin, statesman

Do you know your learning style? My learning style is kinesthetic. I am a hands-on learner. We lead the way we learn, so I lead by teaching people hands-on. A large percentage of people are hands-on learners. After you hire someone and process all the paperwork, the training will begin. It is good to have a mix of reading, practical teaching, and hands-on activities. When you involve others, they learn. That is how it is done. My training consisted of me showing my new employees how to copy a file. Now, you would think that copying a record is super simple, right? Well, it is not rocket science, that's for sure, but there is a way that it needs to be done—especially when dealing with medical records that are exhibited.

I taught my employees the way I was taught. I would show my new hire that you start by copying the file from back to front. This process would keep the records in order from start to finish. For example, Exhibits A to F in order, as they were in the original file. After I showed them how to copy the file by doing it one or two times myself, I then handed it off to them and allowed them to try. I was there with them as they began working on the file. I would stay with them until I knew they were comfortable with all the steps, which included more than just copying. There were other required tasks such as counting the pages, ensuring all the exhibits were in place, signing off the request to copy, indicating on the paperwork what the page count for the file was, packing the file up, mailing it to the attorney, and then finally faxing me the paperwork with hours worked, page count, postage cost, and any issues, if there were any, to note.

I know many small businesses that have no onboarding process at all. Don't be that small business. Train your people so that they can do the job you hired them for. You cannot expect them to be game-ready on a new court without some pre-game training.

My customers are very important to me. In many cases, I say they are number one. But my employees are more important. Without my employees, I could never have built my business. I needed a solid staff to help me take care of all the work that came my way. I was in twenty-seven locations in five states. I promise you, it took people to do the work. Let me ask you a question: Have you ever worked for a difficult person, boss, or manager? I am sure the answer is yes. Don't be that person in your business. Don't let your ego become too big and get the best of you. Humble yourself. Remember, the most powerful and effective leaders are humble. Treat people right, because, without them, you have no business.

I would take good care of my employees. I paid above minimum wage, I gave bonuses, I bought them tires and clothing, and I gave vacations. I even loaned money when needed. More importantly, I encouraged them when I said "thank you" and "good job" since I understood work-life balance. While I was on welfare, I was able to get Dan, the prior owner of STFF, to become what is called a welfare-to-work employer. By being a welfare-to-work employer, he received tax breaks, and I was able to retain my government money and a paycheck. And I promise you, I needed all of it. When I bought the business, not only did I go from welfare to wealth, but I went from being a welfare-to-work participant to being a welfare-to-work employer, and today I train welfare-to-work participants 21st century soft skills. Full circle, my friends, full circle. Because I understood how hard it was being a welfare mom, I did very well with...well...my own kind. Many of the women who worked for me as welfare-to-work workers did so for a very long time. They became *EMPOWERED* under my wing. Then, they flew free.

In welfare, it is common for people to go from job to job. Maintaining a job is difficult. I knew that, and I was able to offer solutions to my staff that taught them how to stay employed, change their lives, and strive for a better life. I was living proof that it could be done, and today I still stand as living proof of that and so much more.

My advice to you is to be open-minded and solution-orientated but understand that many people will say they want to work but only want money. Keep watch for those—they will appear, and if you do hire one or two, remove them as soon as the mask comes off. I promise you will know. Listen to your people. Remember, they are human beings and they have a life outside the workplace. They depend on you to help support their families. Keep lines of communication open. If they do something wrong, nip it in the bud. Don't wait six months down the line to tell them that they messed up six months ago. That is completely unfair. Do performance reviews. Provide additional training and education when needed. Invest in your people and I promise you, they will return the investment threefold.

As I stated earlier, one of the things I do today is train welfare-to-work participants in 21st century soft skills. I also teach those same skills to my students and share them with my clients. Once you go into business, you are going to want to ensure you have a well-rounded staff with employable soft skills.

I want you to think for a moment or two what you think would be the most important 21st century soft skills an employee would need to have. Think about it from the perspective of the business you are building or will build. Think about it from what you have experienced already in the workforce. Then, in the space provided, I want you to list all that comes to mind. I will then reveal to you what the top ten 21st century soft skills are, according to New World of Work.

_____

_____

_____

_____

_____

_____

_____

_____

ENTREPRENEURSHIP EMPOWERED

The information below comes directly from the New World of Work website.

"New World of Work (NWoW) was developed under the Doing What MATTERS for Jobs and the Economy framework of the California Community Colleges system, which is the largest higher education system in the nation with 72 districts and 114 colleges serving 2.1 million students each year. New World of Work is headquartered at Shasta College, a campus dedicated to collaborating with employers, workforce development boards, educators, and research organizations across the country to build college/career-ready, 21st Century Employability Skills. Starting in 2012, the New World of Work team began tracking futurist projections, economic reports, and national research related to the correlation between education and employment. We conducted a series of Skills Panels to gather feedback from employers, entrepreneurs, human resources specialists, educators, and students to determine the essential employability skills required in our emerging global economy. From this, we established our 'Top 10 List of 21st Century Employability Skills.' Expert curriculum developers, including the NWoW Co-Creators, video crews, college faculty across disciplines, and digital badging teams then created lessons and badges to go along with each of our skills.

1. *Adaptability*
2. *Analysis/Solution Mindset*
3. *Collaboration*
4. *Communication*
5. *Digital Fluency*
6. *Entrepreneurial Mindset*
7. *Empathy*
8. *Resilience*
9. *Self-Awareness*
10. *Social/Diversity Awareness"*[25]

Many times, you will be hired for your hard skills but fired for your lack of soft skills. It is critical that you have the soft skills noted—not only in yourself, but your staff needs to have them as well. In our current workforce, we are finding a huge lack of soft skills. You may know how to code, but if you are not able to communicate or work with your co-workers, you will not last in a job. I am now wondering if you had any of the top ten selected as your top soft skills on the list you created earlier. I am sure you had one or two, or perhaps even all ten. When you are looking for solid employees, you want to ensure they come to you with soft skills. What's so exciting about the work I do with NWoW is that they offer digital badges, as explained in the information I shared with you from their website. The digital badges are able to be presented on a person's LinkedIn profile. The ones earned through NWoW have data that backs them and are valid accredited badges. You can create a digital badge; it is very easy to do. But the accreditation part requires work, and a badge is meaningless if nothing backs it.

As a trainer to the trainers for NWoW, I have the honor of doing demo workshops for interested parties. I review the background of NWoW, and then I do the demo lesson. The one I commonly choose is on adaptability. This is mission-critical, especially in the new millennium. Times have changed from when one would go through college, get a degree, then go into a 40-to-50-year career. Those days are over. People will go from one job to the next several times in their life.

Being able to adapt is imperative to being successful in our ever-growing gig economy. That is the economy we are moving into. What is a gig economy? It is a contract labor economy. The term "gig" actually comes from the jazz era. Jazz players would say they had a gig over the weekend, meaning they would be playing at some club or bar. This is where the term originated. As an Empowered Entrepreneur, you will certainly want to consider, and will most likely use, contract labor. For many companies, this is a complete game changer. You don't have to worry about all the paperwork or the hiring process, the training or the waiting around for someone to blossom into their full potential. You simply must go and find what you need by surfing a gig platform like Upwork or even LinkedIn, which, in my professional opinion, is going to be the go-to gig platform, and if you do play the stock game, I'll tell you to consider buying their stock. It is worth checking out. They will certainly be taking over the market.

When hiring gig/contract labor, it is very important to understand they are not your employee, and you are limited on what you may have them do for you. You must have a written scope of work that fully details what they have been retained to do. You will be very clear with descriptions of deliverables and timetables. You will also want to ensure they have some type of professional errors and omission insurance and/or are bonded. You will pay more for contract labor, but more times than not, it will be worth it. What you don't have to worry about with contract labor is taxes, benefits, and any other employment-related cost. Being a contract worker is also a great way to start a business. You may start your business by being a gigger. You may be a photographer and start by doing small jobs here and there, and before you know it, you have a thriving photography business.

As an NWoW trainer, one of my favorite videos to show is the adaptability video by Let It Ripple Film Studio. The video shows how important our human skills are. Even though there are a lot of fears that our technology will grow so much that we, the human, will not be needed and jobs will be lost, this is not true. Yes, technology will grow. I have already told you how important it is for you to be digitally fluent. But I need you to understand that what we need the most in any industry boils down to being human. We need the human skills of curiosity, creativity, taking initiative, multidisciplinary thinking, and empathy—which happen to be skills that machines don't have. Only humans have these skills and, in the words of my dear mentor and friend, Ron Hickey, *"God ensures that our capabilities as humans are matched to His divine calling."* We are in the human economy. You are to support, uplift, and benefit from that economy, starting with yourself. Then you will hire and retain the best of the best.

Your vibrational frequency will be at its highest, and you will not only grow in business, but you will grow in people. Today, I am in the business of building up people who build businesses. Imagine that: a welfare mom, now the CEO of a thriving empire who builds businesses up through seas of people. Human economy, human resources, and human capital—the human is amazing. The Empowered Entrepreneur who fully understands that notion will move from an amazing human to a ridiculously amazing one, and then they will build up others. They will inspire. They will *EMPOWER*, and more importantly, they will leave a legacy and businesses that will live for generations upon generations. They are operating out of the true meaning of "start up to succession." They are in the long game, not the short game, and they care for humans from a place of respect and humility. This is *Entrepreneurship Empowered!*

**Chapter 9**: Launch, Manage, and Grow

"Step out of the history that is holding you back. Step into the new story you are willing to create."

—Oprah Winfrey, business tycoon

In *Entrepreneurship Empowered*, we don't predict our future using history; we create it by going to the ultra-limits of our lives by believing in our natural talents and abilities, which have been bestowed upon us by God. By now, I am hoping you have been able to discover more of who you are. The prior chapters have weaved in and out of self-awareness. Because it all boils down to "self." No matter which way you look or go, at the core is "self." Many times, you need to get out of your own way. I want you to imagine, if you will, a bird perched on a pier railing resting upon the seashore. The most beautifully colored blue and gray wings raised, ready for flight, but little yellow feet still stuck to the railing. The bird is ready for flight, but if it doesn't release its grip from the railing and activate its wings, it will only stand there looking silly with its wings up. My questions to you are: Are you ready to take flight? Do you know where you are going? Are you prepared? If your answers are "no," then you need to get to work. But if your answers are "yes," what then are you waiting for? Why are your wings up but feet stuck to the ground? Is it fear of failure? Which, mind you, we make up. There really is no failure. Falling on your face is fantastic; I encourage it. Faith is dead without works, but if you do the work, don't let your faith die because of fear. Many people do the work and work hard, but then never activate their wings and launch because they fear falling on their face.

I have a friend who is part of a wonderful community I am in. He lost his legs in the military. Today he is a speaker and a phenomenal one at that. He tells the story of when he got his new legs, how the doctor began working with him. His very first therapy session with his new legs was not what he was expecting, to say the least. The rails he held onto as he moved forward, step by step, disappeared into the ground. The minute they disappeared into the ground and he had nothing to hold on to, he fell forward and landed on his face. He was so angry with the doctor. He said to the doctor, *"See, I told you this wasn't going to work, I just fell on my face. You don't know what you're doing."* The doctor said, *"I am teaching you how to walk, now get up and let's try this again."* Today, this same man doesn't just walk, but he runs marathons, triathlons, and a host of other very challenging sporting events. But first, he had to fall flat on his face.

Many of you desire to be an Empowered Entrepreneur, but you fear falling on your face. Don't do yourself an injustice. Don't throw away all the time you spent working on a business model or plan and put your wings up only to stay stuck to the ground because you fear falling. Falling is a part of the process. You need to fall. You don't learn by hitting the bullseye; you learn by missing the mark. And you will never learn if you don't release your grip and activate your wings.

There is a lot that goes into launching a business. You will want to pick a location. I am sure you have heard the saying before: "location, location, location." Location is important, depending on what industry you are in. For me, it wasn't about the location, though I had twenty-seven different locations at my peak. Those locations were already established for me because I provided a service in the Social Security Administration. For my tanning salon, however, I was connected to a gym. Though I was the only tanning salon in the area, I was in a plaza that didn't have much traffic, other than the gym, which didn't pull much traffic for me at all. After I bought the tanning salon, I realized that was why the gym owners wanted to sell it. It wasn't generating the money it needed to, so selling it was the better option for them.

I was young in my entrepreneurship, and I didn't do the research I now teach all my students and clients to do. You certainly want to do your research when it comes to location, and you will need to pay special attention to the local zoning ordinances and the taxes. There may even be some state, local, and federal incentives for you to bring a new business into an area. Economic development is big, and that is where the incentives will often come from.

You will need to be sure you pick a business structure before launching your business. We discussed them in earlier chapters, but I know they can be very perplexing. I highly recommend you work with an attorney or an accountant when deciding on what business legal structure you select. I was, and still am, a sole proprietor. However, as I move forward, I will become incorporated.

What I need you to understand the most about the business legal structure is the liability part. When you are a sole proprietor, all the liability is yours, not the business's. You and the business are one. You have no protection over your personal assets. You will need to carefully assess your current and future risks. Be very wise when selecting your legal structure, and make sure to ask all the questions you need. Knowledge is powerful, and you will need all that you can acquire, not only for success in business, but for success in life.

Because the business structures are perplexing, I have defined them again for you below. These definitions come directly from SBA.

- *"A sole proprietorship is a business that is owned and usually operated by one person. It is the oldest, simplest, and cheapest form of business ownership because there is no legal distinction made between the owner and the business.*
- *A partnership is two or more people voluntarily operating a business as co-owners for profit. Partnerships make up more than 8 percent of all businesses in the United States and more than 11 percent of the total revenue.*
- *A C corporation is an artificial person created by law, with most of the legal rights of a real person. These include the rights to start and operate a business, to buy or sell property, to borrow money, to sue or be sued, and to enter into binding contracts. Corporations make up 20 percent of all businesses in the United States, but they account for almost 90 percent of the revenue.*
- *S corporations are corporations that elect to pass corporate income, losses, deductions, and credits through to their shareholders for federal tax purposes. Shareholders of S corporations report the flow-through of income and losses on their personal tax returns and are assessed tax at their individual income tax rates. This allows S corporations to avoid double taxation on the corporate income. S corporations are responsible for tax on certain built-in gains and passive income at the entity level.*
- *The limited liability company is a relatively new form of business ownership that is now permitted in all fifty states, although the laws of each state may*

differ. The LLC is a blend of a sole proprietorship and a corporation: the owners of the LLC have limited liability and are taxed only once for the business."[15]

Early in the book, I promised you some steps that you can take to form an LLC. Well, as promised, here are steps you need to take according to Nolo:

1. "***Choose an LLC name.*** *The name of your business cannot be the same as the name of another limited liability company (LLC) on file with your state's LLC office (which is usually part of the same division as corporations, often the Secretary of State's office). The name must end with an LLC designator, such as "Limited Liability Company" or "Limited Company," or an abbreviation of one of these phrases ("LLC," "L.L.C.," or "Ltd. Liability Co.").*

2. ***File articles of organization.*** *Prepare and file "articles of organization" with your state's LLC filing office. Typically, you must provide only your LLC's name, its address, and sometimes the names of all of the owners—called members.*

3. ***Create an LLC operating agreement.*** *The LLC operating agreement contains rules for the ownership and operation of the business (much like a partnership agreement or corporate bylaws). A typical operating agreement includes the members' percentage interests in the business, the members' rights and responsibilities, and information on voting, management, and profits and losses.*

4. ***Publish a notice (AZ and NY only).*** *This step does not apply to LLCs in most states. If you are forming an LLC in Arizona or New York, you must take an additional step to make your company official: You must publish in a local newspaper a notice stating that you intend to form an LLC. Your local newspaper should be able to help you with this filing.*

5. ***Obtain licenses and permits.*** *Before you begin doing business, you need to obtain the required licenses and permits that anyone needs to start a new business. Among the licenses and permits you may need to obtain are a business license and, if your LLC will sell products, a seller's permit.*

6. *Retain your limited liability.* *To retain your LLC's status as a separate entity, LLC owners (members) must observe certain formalities, such as keeping detailed financial records and recording minutes of major decisions.*"[26]

You will need to be sure that you have not only a business structure selected, but also a business name to be registered. For me, the business I bought had a name. All I needed to do was register that I was now doing business as (DBA) Start To Finish Files. If you purchase a business that has an existing name, you will need to do the same. Once you get your DBA (**D**oing **B**usiness **A**s; see below), you will then be able to open a bank account in the business name, which is very important. I will cover more on this later. First, there are four ways to register your name:

1. Entity name
2. Trademark
3. Doing Business As (DBA) name
4. Domain name

The following information comes directly from the SBA: "*An entity name can protect the name of your business at a state level. Depending on your business structure and location, the state may require you to register a legal entity name. Your entity name is how the state identifies your business. Each state may have different rules about what your entity name can be and usage of company suffixes. Most states don't allow you to register a name that's already been registered by someone else, and some states require your entity name to reflect the kind of business it represents. In most cases, your entity name registration protects your business and prevents anyone else in the state from operating under the same entity name. However, there are exceptions pertaining to state and business structure. Check with your state for rules about how to register your business name.*

A trademark can protect the name of your business, goods, and services at a national level. Trademarks prevent others in the same (or similar) industry in the U.S. from using your trademarked names. For example, if you were an electronics company and wanted to call your business Springfield Electronic Accessories and one of your products Screen Cover 5000, trademarking those names would prevent other electronics businesses or similar products from using those same names. Businesses in every state are subject to trademark infringement lawsuits, which can prove costly. That's why you should check your prospective business, product, and service names against the official trademark database, maintained by the United States Patent and Trademark Office.

You might need to register your DBA—also known as a trade name, fictitious name, or assumed name—with the state, county, or city your business is located in. Registering your DBA name doesn't provide legal protection by itself, but most states require you to register your DBA if you use one. Some business structures require you to use a DBA. Even if you're not required to register a DBA, you might want to anyway. A DBA lets you conduct business under a different identity from your own personal name or your formal business entity name. As an added bonus, getting a DBA and federal tax ID number (EIN) allows you to open a business bank account. Multiple businesses can go by the same DBA in one state, so you're less restricted in what you can choose. There's also more leeway in the clarity of business function. For example, a small business owner could use Springfield Electronic Accessories for their entity name but use TechBuddy for their DBA. Just remember that trademark infringement laws will still apply. Determine your DBA requirements based on your specific location. Requirements vary by business structure as well as by state, county, and municipality, so check with local government offices and websites.

If you want an online presence for your business, start by registering a domain name—also known as your website address, or URL. Once you register your domain name, no one else can use it for as long as you continue to own it. It's a good way to protect your brand presence online. If someone else has already registered the domain you wanted to use, that's okay. Your domain name doesn't actually need to be the same as your legal business name, trademark, or DBA. For example, Springfield Electronic Accessories could register the domain name techbuddyspringfield.com. You'll register your domain name through a registrar service. Consult a directory of accredited registrars to determine which ones are safe to use, and then pick one that offers you the best combination of price and customer service. You'll need to renew your domain registration on a regular basis.

The next part of launching your business is obtaining your Employer Identification Number (EIN), which is your federal tax ID. You need it to pay federal taxes, hire employees, open a bank account, and apply for business licenses and permits. It's free to apply for an EIN, and you should do it right after you register your business. Your business needs a federal tax ID number if it does any of the following:

- Pays employees
- Operates as a corporation or partnership
- Files tax returns for employment, excise, or alcohol, tobacco, and firearms
- Withholds taxes on income, other than wages, paid to a non-resident alien
- Uses a Keogh Plan (a tax-deferred pension plan)
- Works with certain types of organizations

Apply for an EIN with the IRS assistance tool. It will guide you through questions and ask for your name, social security number, address, and your 'Doing Business As' (DBA) name. Your nine-digit federal tax ID becomes available immediately upon verification.

Next comes the licenses and permits if needed. You'll need to get a federal license or permit if your business activities are regulated by a federal agency. Check to see if any of your business activities are listed here, and then check with the right federal agency to see how to apply.

Requirements and fees depend on your business activity and the agency issuing the license or permit. It's best to check with the issuing agency for details on the business license cost. SBA gives you a beautiful chart that directs you where to go for permits. The licenses and permits you need from the state, county, or city will depend on your business activities and business location. Your business license fees will also vary.

States tend to regulate a broader range of activities than the federal government. For example, business activities that are commonly regulated locally include auctions, construction, and dry cleaning, farming, plumbing, restaurants, retail, and vending machines. Some licenses and permits expire after a set period of time. Keep close track of when you need to renew them—it's often easier to renew than it is to apply for a new one. You'll have to research your own state, county, and city regulations. Industry requirements often vary by state. Visit your state's website to find out which permits and licenses you need.

You will also need to get a business bank account. As soon as you start accepting or spending money as your business, you should open a business bank account. Common business accounts include a checking account, savings account, credit card account, and a merchant services account. Merchant services accounts allow you to accept credit and debit card transactions from your customers. You can open a business bank account once you've gotten your federal EIN. Most business bank accounts offer perks that don't come with a standard personal bank account.

- Protection. Business banking offers limited personal liability protection by keeping your business funds separate from your personal funds. Merchant services also offer purchase protection for your customers and ensures that their personal information is secure.
- Professionalism. Customers will be able to pay you with credit cards and make checks out to your business instead of directly to you. Plus, you'll be able

185

to authorize employees to handle day-to-day banking tasks on behalf of the business.
- *Preparedness. Business banking usually comes with the option for a line of credit for the company. This can be used in the event of an emergency, or if your business needs new equipment.*
- *Purchasing power. Credit card accounts can help your business make large startup purchases and help establish a credit history for your business.*

Opening a business bank account is easy once you've picked your bank. Simply go online or to a local branch to begin the process. Here are some of the most common documents banks ask for when you open a business bank account. Some banks may ask for more.

- *Employer Identification Number (EIN) (or a Social Security number, if you're a sole proprietorship)*
- *Your business's formation documents*
- *Ownership agreements*
- *Business license"*[15]

Make sure you are prepared when going to the bank to set up your account, and, as always, do your research on which bank is best for you. Personally, I have my business account with a credit union. The man I bought my business from helped me set up my business account with Patelco Credit Union, and it has been a great place for all my banking needs in business and in my personal accounts. Do your research.

You will also need to research the different types of insurance you will need to have. Some industries require particular types of insurance, and without that type of insurance, you will not be able to conduct business. Make sure you know your industry and what is required. The following information comes directly from the SBA.

There are six common types of insurance:

1. "**General liability insurance**
   a. *Any business.*

ENTREPRENEURSHIP EMPOWERED

     b. *This coverage protects against financial loss as the result of bodily injury, property damage, medical expenses, libel, slander, defending lawsuits, and settlement bonds or judgments.*

2. **Product liability insurance**
     a. *Businesses that manufacture, wholesale, distribute, and retail a product.*
     b. *This coverage protects against financial loss as a result of a defective product that causes injury or bodily harm.*

3. **Professional liability insurance**
     a. *Businesses that provide services to customers.*
     b. *This coverage protects against financial loss as a result of malpractice, errors, and negligence.*

4. **Commercial property insurance**
     a. *Businesses with a significant amount of property and physical assets.*
     b. *This coverage protects your business against loss and damage of company property due to a wide variety of events such as fire, smoke, wind and hail storms, civil disobedience and vandalism.*

5. **Home-based business insurance**
     a. *Businesses that are run out of the owner's personal home.*
     b. *Coverage that's added to homeowner's insurance as a rider can offer protection for a small amount of business equipment and liability coverage for third-party injuries.*

6. **Business owner's policy**
     a. *Most small business owners, but especially home-based business owners.*
     b. *A business owner's policy is an insurance package that combines all of the typical coverage options into one bundle. They simplify the insurance buying process and can save you money.*

There are four steps to buying business insurance:

1. ***Assess your risks***. Think about what kind of accidents, natural disasters, or lawsuits could damage your business. If you need help, the National Federation of Independent Businesses (NFIB) provides information for choosing insurance to help you assess your risks and to make sure you've insured every aspect of your business.
2. ***Find a reputable licensed agent***. Commercial insurance agents can help you find policies that match your business needs. They receive commissions from insurance companies when they sell policies, so it's important to find a licensed agent that's interested in your needs as much as his/her own.
3. ***Shop around***. Prices and benefits can vary significantly. You should compare rates, terms, and benefits for insurance offers from several different agents.
4. ***Reassess every year***. As your business grows, so do your liabilities. If you have purchased or replaced equipment or expanded operations, you should contact your insurance agent to discuss changes in your business and how they affect your coverage."[15]

"Managing a business, small or large, today requires an extremely disciplined, thoughtful approach with regard to the pressure that people are under."

—Howard Schultz, CEO of Starbucks

Now that you are all planned up, ready to launch, and have released your grip from the railing and your wings are activated, your next move is to manage the flight. You will need to manage time and money the closest. They are the two biggest concerns in business, outside of employees. Getting a handle on time and understanding why you do what you do with your time is just as important as getting a handle on your spending habits and what you do with your money.

Let's start with time. Poor time management can cause us so much stress, which can be the demise of your business. Small businesses cannot afford to waste time on bad time management and inefficiency. Bad time management is often one of the greatest downfalls of small businesses. The necessity of having solid time management skills and practices is immeasurable. An Empowered Entrepreneur who utilizes good time management is much better positioned to consistently deliver their product or service on time. I always recommend to my students, and even to my clients who struggle with time management, that they take a project management course. Project management teaches you so much on how to handle time, particularly when dealing with projects.

In project management, one of the top techniques you will learn is backwards planning. Through this technique, you start at your end/due date and work backwards. You will always have a set time that is called your margin of error time. To err is human, and emergencies happen. You must be able to handle both. Plan for it. When I have a due date, I always plan to have my deliverable done at least two or three days prior to the deadline date. If you are a person who waits till the last minute, you will need to change that behavior prior to running and working your business—or you will be the demise of your business because you manage your time poorly.

The best way to manage your money is to come to the truth of what you do with it. I mentioned in Chapter Six that I make all my students track their money. I make them do this because if you don't know how to manage your personal money, you will struggle with managing a business's money. Money can become a master, just like technology, so you must be careful with it and remember that you are in control. Once you take a closer look at your spending habits and become wise with your money by learning how to curb your appetite for foolish spending, you will be able to take your wisdom and place it in your business.

It is wise to bring in help with your financial matters. Consider hiring a certified public accountant (CPA) or bookkeeper, or use an online service. A CPA will typically cost more than online services but can normally offer more tailored services for your specific business needs. A bookkeeper can provide basic day-to-day functions at a lower cost but won't possess the formal accounting education of a CPA. Ensure that someone can manage the following:

- *Accounts receivable*
- *Accounts payable*
- *Available cash*
- *Bank reconciliation*
- *Payroll*

You will also need to manage your business credit. Establishing and managing business credit can help your company secure financing when you need it, and with better terms. Business credit can be crucial for negotiating supply agreements and protecting against business identity theft. The SBA shares five steps that can lay the groundwork to sound financial planning:

1. *"Determine whether you have business credit on file with Dun & Bradstreet*
2. *Establish a business credit history by using lines of credit associated with your business*
3. *Pay bills on time and understand other factors that influence your credit rating*
4. *Keep your credit files current and monitor for ratings changes*
5. *Know your customers' and vendors' credit standing*

Knowing your customers' credit standing gives you a window into consumer patterns, and that can affect your marketing and sales strategy. You may not need to conduct credit checks, but there are credit evaluation tools available for small business. Customer behavior also impacts your business's cash flow, which affects planning for future supplies, hiring employees, and expanding your business."[15]

"The best executive is the one who has sense enough to pick good men to do what he wants done, and self-restraint to keep from meddling with them while they do it."

—Theodore Roosevelt, former U.S. president

Managing your human capital can be very challenging, but ever so rewarding at the same time. I love what Roosevelt's quote above states at the end. Basically, he is saying that you must not meddle with your employees. You hired them to do a job. For goodness' sake, let them do that damn job. Oftentimes, managers and leaders don't trust their employees to do their job, so they micromanage. This is a waste of time and money. In my main business, my employees worked independently. After I trained them up, I let them go and they worked by themselves, unsupervised. They worked in other cities and states, so I was not able to be right beside them, checking to see if they were doing the work correctly. I had to trust that they were. I had to have confidence in my ability to train and lead, which I did and still do today.

Communication is big in managing your employees. You need to listen to them. Finding out what their needs are is so very helpful—not only to them, but to you as well. I spent much time in Chapter Eight covering human resources and how to handle it properly. If you need to, go back and review that chapter. What I want you to understand is that you are responsible for your people. They are under your care when they work for you. Be good to them. Listen to them. *EMPOWER* them. Some of the basic things you will handle with regard to management are their work schedules, workloads, unexpected emergencies, human tragedies such as death or illness, paying them, and allowing them vacation or time off—just to name a few. Each business will be different in its dealings with its employees.

Outside of managing your time, money, and employees, you will need to manage your taxes and stay compliant. The following information comes directly from the SBA:

*"Your business is legally required to pay taxes and keep accounting records on a consistent yearly schedule called a tax year. Most businesses choose their tax year to be the same as the calendar year. You select your tax year the first time you file for taxes, but you can change it later with permission from the IRS. Calendar tax year if you don't have special accounting needs for your business. Fiscal tax year if you want your 12-month accounting cycle to end in a month that isn't December. Short tax year if your business wasn't in existence for an entire tax year, or you changed your accounting period. If your business doesn't have much reporting or bookkeeping, you might be required to use a calendar tax year. Check with the IRS for detailed rules about tax years. Your business might need to pay state and local taxes. Tax laws vary by location and business structure, so you'll need to check with state and local governments to know your business' tax obligations. The two most common types of **state and local** tax requirements for small business are income taxes and employment taxes. Your state income tax obligations are determined by your business structure. For example, corporations are taxed separately from the owners, while sole proprietors report their personal and business income taxes using the same form. If your business has employees, you'll be responsible for paying state employment taxes. These vary by state but often include workers' compensation insurance, unemployment insurance taxes, and temporary disability insurance. You might also be responsible for withholding employee income tax. Check with your state tax authority to find out how much you need to withhold and when you need to send it to the state. Your business structure determines what federal taxes you must pay and how you pay them. Some of the taxes require payment throughout the year, so it's important to know your tax obligations before the end of your tax year.*

There are five general types of business taxes:

1. Income tax
2. Self-employment tax
3. Estimated tax
4. Employer tax
5. Excise tax

Each category of business tax might have special rules, qualifications, or IRS forms you need to file. Check with the IRS to see which business taxes apply to you.

If your business has employees, you might be required to withhold taxes from their paychecks. Federal employment taxes include income, Social Security and Medicare, unemployment, and self-employment taxes. Check with the IRS to see which taxes you need to withhold.

Corporations have the strictest internal requirements. Corporations should hold initial and annual director and shareholder meetings, record their meeting minutes, adopt and maintain bylaws, issue stock to shareholders, and record all stock transfers.

LLCs have less strict internal requirements but are generally advised to maintain an updated operating agreement, issue membership shares, record all membership interest transfers, and hold annual meetings. Other business structures have few, if any, internal requirements. However, it's rarely a bad idea to document important decisions with your business. Your annual filing requirements will vary based on your business structure and the state. Still, there are a few common requirements to look out for.

Annual report or biennial statement. Most states require one or the other. Some states set the due date on the anniversary of the business formation date, and other states pick a specific day for all businesses. Statement filing fees. Fees normally accompany the annual report or biennial statement, which can exceed $300.00. Franchise tax. Some states charge franchise taxes for corporations or LLCs that operate within their borders. Formulas vary by state. Initial reports. *Some states require initial reports and fees shortly after incorporation. Articles of Amendment. If you've made important changes to your company—like address, name, new shares, or membership—report it with articles of amendment. The documents for staying legally compliant vary based on your industry and location. Maintain any licenses, permits, or certificates your business received from your state, city, or county. Renewal requirements vary, so it's best to check with local business licensing offices."*[15]

As I am sure you can see, there is a lot that goes into running and managing a business, but this is not all there is. You will also need to manage your assets, equipment, and all other expenses that it will take to operate your business. Then you will need to manage the marketing and the sales portion of your business.

Can you see now how having a team is super beneficial? If you expect to grow, it is mandatory. First and foremost, you are the team. You will need to learn how to manage all parts of your business and fall flat on your face in many areas. Like I stated at the beginning of this chapter, it is perfectly okay to fall flat on your face. What I don't want you to do is stay there. Get up, dust yourself off, and make adjustments. Take a 360-degree look at your business and at yourself. Understand what you are good at, where you need to grow, and where you need to hire in order to move your business forward. It is not a lone wolf production from start to finish. And many times, the people you start with are not the ones you finish with. Look at Ronald McDonald—he had a whole host of friends at the beginning, but now it is just him. I am kind of like Ronald McDonald. I had a full staff doing all kinds of things, but now it is just me. It surely was a good thing that I knew how to handle all aspects of my business, because once I had no more employees, the workload decreased. I was left with only me.

"Strength and growth come only through continuous effort and struggle."

—Napoleon Hill, *Think and Grow Rich*

Growing my business was so exciting. It took continuous effort, no question. And it wasn't easy. I was, however, very strategic in growth. I had a vision, and I stuck with it. When I purchased my business, Dan told me there was an opportunity to expand into Southern California. He chose not to grow that direction because of all the effort that was required, but he left me with the seed of growth...and I took it, watered it, and cared for it. I am a farmer with a very green thumb. Before I could blink an eye, I had grown from six locations in half a state to twenty-seven locations in five states. See the timeline for how I grew:

- 2002 Northern California (6)
  - Sacramento, Stockton, San Rafael, San Francisco, San Jose, and Oakland
- 2003 Santa Barbara (7)
- 2004 Southern California (14)
  - Los Angeles, Los Angeles West, Orange, Downey, San Diego, Pasadena, and Long Beach
- 2006 Arizona and Nevada (17)
  - Tucson, Phoenix, and Las Vegas
- 2007 Georgia and Florida (27)
  - Atlanta, Atlanta North, Augusta, Macon, Jacksonville, Orlando, Tampa, Ft. Myers, Ft. Lauderdale, and Miami

I grew in locations, but there are other ways to grow. Perhaps you may grow in products or different types of services you offer. Regardless of which way you grow, please understand that it will take effort, and you must be committed. You must remember that you are in the long game, not the short game. It will take money to grow your business. For me, I bootstrapped my entire growth, meaning I self-supported the growth. But many small businesses will seek funding to help grow their business. You will need to ensure you can provide any investor or bank with solid numbers, and that growth is on the horizon. You must be invested in your business and have a stake in it before anyone else will invest in you.

If you do begin to grow into other locations as I did, you will need to make sure you research the market in the new locations, the permits required to conduct business, if any are needed, and the taxes that are required, as each state has different tax requirements. For me, I was a service provided, so once again, growing into my locations looked a bit different than the average small business. I am a big believer in claiming what is mine. One of the first things I did was have magnets made up. It was a magnet of the United States, and on it was my logo. I claimed the U.S. in that very moment, and if paper was still around in my industry, I would not be writing this book right now—I would be out in the U.S. somewhere gobbling up more business.

Because I am action-oriented, the next thing that I did was walk inside every single office I declared was mine. Upon setting my foot on the ground, I claimed it. It was mine, and guess what—I got exactly what I claimed: abundance everywhere, business everywhere, and growth upon growth. I also visited new and existing clients in person and brought them gifts, such as flowers, T-shirts with my logo on them, coffee cups...the list goes on and on. Most of my business was done virtually, so them being able to put a face to the name and the service was the icing on the cake.

The human element—I will continue to tell you time and time again—is the key that opens the door. This is my truth. Remember, in *Entrepreneurship Empowered*, we don't predict our future; we create it. And I not only create it, I claim it, and it does manifest. I surrender my grip and I activate my wings and I fly. You are perfectly capable of doing the same. The power resides in your mind. It is up to you to release the grip and fly.

Another way I grew my business was by becoming a federal contractor. There are many federal contracts that go untapped. It amazes me how many. In the chambers of the

Social Security Administration, there are hearing monitors who are basically court reporters. They record the hearings on a digital recording system and computer. I bid on the contract and won. It was a $1.5 million contract to be paid over a five-year period. My business had just grown in a different type of service. Now I could provide court reporting services. Keep in mind, according to the SBA: *"The U.S. government is the world's largest customer. It buys all types of products and services and is required by law to provide opportunities for small businesses. There are two broad categories of government contractors:*

- ***Prime contractors** bid on and win contracts directly from government agencies*
- ***Subcontractors** join prime contractor teams, usually to provide a specific capability or product*

For your small business to serve as a prime contractor or subcontractor, you'll need to legally qualify as a small business and register as a government contractor. Then you can start looking for both prime and sub-contracting opportunities with the federal government. The federal government tries to award a significant percentage of all federal government contracting dollars to small businesses. In addition, the federal government tries to award a certain percentage to businesses in the following categories.

- *Women-owned small businesses*
- *Small disadvantaged business*
- *Service-disabled veteran-owned small businesses*
- *HUBZone program participants*

The SBA's 8(a) Business Development program helps eligible socially and economically disadvantaged individuals grow their businesses through one-on-one counseling, training workshops, matchmaking opportunities with federal buyers, and other management and technical guidance."[15]

I have stated it time and time again: do your research. The SBA is a great place to start looking for information that will help you grow your business. Remember that as an Empowered Entrepreneur, you are playing the long game, not the short game. Growth comes, but your seed may have to die before it will come back and give you the best crop ever. You will struggle, and you will get tired, but what I need for you to do is never give up.

As we begin to wrap up our journey together in my closing chapter, I will be moving us forward to all the important *Palumbo Principles*, which I want you to keep on you at all times. More so, I need you to crawl deeply into yourself. Write your vision and run with it. I know people may think you are crazy—shoot, even you may think you are crazy—but the difference between genius and insanity is self-awareness, especially when doing something over and over again, expecting different results.

Thomas Edison was very aware of himself. He was told by teachers, friends, colleagues, and the like that he was crazy, he was ignorant, he was a failure. Then, he created the light bulb, and all of a sudden, he became a genius. But I beg to differ; he was always a genius. It wasn't the light bulb that made him one. The light bulb was simply a byproduct of his authentic self being exactly who he was designed to be, which was to create. And today, we have light everywhere.

# Chapter 10: The 10 Core Palumbo Principles

"I love those who can smile in trouble, who can gather strength from distress, and grow brave by reflection. 'Tis the business of little minds to shrink, but they whose heart is firm, and whose conscience approves their conduct, will pursue their principles unto death."

—Leonardo da Vinci, Renaissance genius

As an artist myself, I admire the work of Leonardo da Vinci. Not to mention he is Italian like me, which I also love. The quote above is right on the money. I am leaving you now with this final chapter, *The 10 Core Palumbo Principles*, which I personally pursue unto death. In building my final empire, which is the Eternal Enterprise, I capture eternal life, and no longer will these principles be pursued only unto death. But I am confident they will be shared with the world, and more importantly, they will guide my seeds into seeds forevermore. This, my friends, is how you not only break generational curses, this is how you plant generational blessings.

Before I share the 10 Core Palumbo Principles, I would like to sincerely thank you for reading this far. My prayer is that you not only received a wealth of information that you will use to become the most incredible Empowered Entrepreneur around, but that you have received inspiration for your own personal journey. It took me many years to finally pull the muzzle off my mouth and live out loud. I have an extraordinary God-given talent, which is to give others a very special gift: the gift of self. Yes, you read that correctly. I give you the tools to find yourself. And, in doing so, I have given you everything you need. Like a domino effect, after you truly grasp hold of the gift of you, everything else will fall into place. As you read the final words of this book, I encourage you to take time when reading. Deeply digest. Ponder. Reflect. And give way to the future.

Palumbo Principle 10: Pay Yourself First!

As an Empowered Entrepreneur, I need you to understand that you must pay yourself first. So often, clients and students come to me during the process of working on the financial part of the business—and far too often, they fail to add their salaries in there. Whether you have the money to pay yourself or not doesn't matter. You still need to allocate the money, and then when you do have the actual funds on hand, you compensate yourself. Paying yourself first, however, doesn't start in business, but rather in your personal life. You must pay yourself first. You should always take your paycheck and put a percentage of the money away for yourself—a savings, if you will. It doesn't have to be a lot; just make sure you take something and put it away. *"But Professor, my lights are due, and so is the rent. I only have enough to pay that."* I understand, but guess what? You must be disciplined and still put some money away for you. You need to have a "come-to-Jesus" moment with yourself and take a cold, hard look at your money, and even more so, your spending habits. You don't have a salary problem; you have a spending problem. When you pay yourself first, you are teaching yourself that saving is a priority and important to your future. You must know that you are worth paying yourself first.

Find yourself a bank that offers a high-interest savings account and open one for yourself. Have your money deposited into that account and only pull out what you need. Leave the rest. Another suggestion is to simply have a certain amount of your money taken out and placed in a savings account or retirement fund. That way, when you get your check, it is what it is, and you don't have to worry about taking ANY additional money out. Many companies will take money out for you.

Here's another option: many banks will automatically move a certain amount of money for you from checking to savings. Even if you start by saving 1% of your income, you will have started saving. We can all save 1% of our income. Come on now, right? You just need to stop spending 10% of it on wasteful things, which you will discover you do. Just track your money and you will see what I am talking about. Again, you don't have a salary issue, you have a spending issue.

Trying to keep up with the Joneses is an old saying, and you may have heard it before—however, this is the new millennium, so people are trying to keep up with the Kardashians now. Both the Joneses and the Kardashians are illusions. That is not your life, so stop trying to keep up with them. They, too, have their problems and issues. Money doesn't change that. Mindset does. I need you to have an abundant mindset and realize everything you need already exists and is available to you. I want you to practice the abundant mindset by giving gratitude for all you desire and all you have. Be wise with your abundance. Some of you need to stop supporting other people's dreams while yours die a slow death. Some of you need to let go of bad habits that have overtaken your bank accounts. Many of you need to stop eating out so damn much and learn to eat what you have.

Once you become wise with your money, you learn to give gratitude for your abundance. Then your cup will overflow. And when it does, you, my friend, are the first one to get paid. Got that? **Pay Yourself First!**

Palumbo Principle 9: Emotional Intelligence Is Key

You have heard me tell you several times throughout this book how important EQ is. For me, it was a complete game changer. It started on a personal level. I have shared small parts of my story with you, and you are aware that I come from a background of intense trauma. Well, this trauma gave me a ton of side effects, one of which was wounded emotion. Wounded emotion will win time and time again against logic. Even though your logic is undeniable, it doesn't, nor will it ever, matter to wounded emotion. EQ, on the other hand, will always give way to logic, and it holds great space for emotion but doesn't allow you to stay trapped in emotion. You must exchange your wounded emotion for EQ. When you do, you will be mentally and emotionally stronger, and a much healthier person overall.

How do you do that, you may ask? First, you must acknowledge that you need help. That you, too, like everyone else on this crazy place called earth, have some issues that need to be dealt with, and you refuse to die with them. You then reach out and find some therapy and pursue self-awareness, personal development, and knowledge like they're a billion dollars just waiting to be had.

Secondly, find help. There are many resources out there for you. You can do a Google search and come up with a thousand and one resources. The therapy I highly suggest is EMDR. What is EMDR? EMDR is defined by the EMDR institute as *"Eye Movement Desensitization and Reprocessing. It is a psychotherapy treatment that was originally designed to alleviate the distress associated with traumatic memories."* For me, this is the most powerful therapy I have encountered. I use this type of therapy, as well as sand tray and art therapy, to help me heal and be free. But again, it starts by acknowledging the need. It starts by saying, "*I am done carrying this weight, this sham. I am tired of dancing with a wounded emotion, and I deserve to be emotionally intelligent.*"

EQ is not only understanding self, but it is also understanding how and why others do what they do. How to better interact with others. How to lead and manage others more effectively. How to understand and serve the needs of society as a whole. Those of us with higher EQ are more authentic in nature and more controlled. You need both of these as you build and develop your business, but more so when you are working with and serving others. The more you can learn about EQ and the more emotionally intelligent you become, the greater success you will have in life and in business. Imagine, if you will for a moment, that the world as a whole was much more emotionally intelligent. I can only imagine how much more effective we would be.

One of my favorite emotional intelligence experts is Ashley Zahabian. She discovered EQ through her own struggle with severe anorexia. Today, she is one of the most powerful speakers and leadership experts known in the U.S. and around the world. One of the elements of EQ that she really goes into is delayed gratification. What is delayed gratification? It is waiting for something better. Saying "no" now because your "YES" is so much better. Saying, "*No, I don't want that marshmallow, because you told me if I eat that one now, I don't get another one later. And if I deny myself eating it now, then I get two later.*" It means going to the gym today and every day, staying consistent because you know that the results will come. It means that when you are paying yourself first, you take that money and save it for later. You deny yourself right now because your gratification for what is to come is so much better. I am in the business of building up people who build businesses, but every business should be building up people. Building people requires delayed gratification. It takes patience, regulating and controlling of emotion, and effective leadership—all of which require emotional intelligence. In *Entrepreneurship*

Empowered, you must have a very high EQ, and you must remain gritty always.

Palumbo Principle 8: Stay Gritty, Baby

One of the best compliments I ever received was that I was gritty. Now, mind you, I had no clue what the hell that meant at first. I was like, *"Huh, I have grit in my teeth?"* *(SMILE)* But then the granter of such a wonderful compliment went on to tell me what grit was. Grit is defined as *"passion and perseverance over a long period of time for goals."* Then he proceeded to tell me, "Stay gritty, baby," and that is exactly what I did and will continue to do. There really is no finish line, you see. Goals are achieved, and new ones are born. We play the long game, not the short game. Being gritty is tightly aligned with a growth mindset, which I shared at the very beginning of this book as the one theme that tied all Empowered Entrepreneurs together. We have a growth mindset. In essence, we are gritty.

I pursued my MBA (**M**aster's in **B**usiness **A**dministration) not only to become a better businesswoman, but also to be able to teach at the community college. I graduated in 2010, and I didn't get my first college teaching job until 2015. I pursued the college professor goal for five years. I also lost over a hundred pounds. It took over a year to lose that weight. A hundred pounds is not easy to lose. That, my friends, is a lot of weight to carry, and a lot of weight to get rid of. I had to use a lot of self-denial and delayed gratification. Every day, I had to stick with my meal prep, my workout regimen, and my mental health. With health and with life, it boils down to a formula: 80% mental, 19% food, and 1% workout. I had to be mentally strong. Being emotionally intelligent helped me be mentally strong. I had to prep my food and eat it daily. I had to drink my water and a lot of it. I had to say "no" to many things, including people. Then, after a little over a year, I went from a size 24 to a size 8, and from just under 300 pounds to 179 pounds.

In business, I am just as gritty. As I have stated before, I grew my business from six locations to twenty-seven locations. From half a state to five states. From a hundred clients to more than five hundred law firms. It required all the principles I have shared with you thus far, and then some. I knew that I was going to have whatever I desired. I just had to be willing to work hard. That is grit. Grit is hard work. Grit is saying, *"No matter how intelligent or skilled I may be, doesn't always matter. But if I don't give up, if I continue to work hard, I will succeed."* Guess what happens when you work hard? Your intellect increases, your skills improve, and you become an unstoppable beast.

You will need to be gritty your entire life. Yes, even unto death. You see, gritty people have hope—they are optimistic for the future. I promise that to understand and have hope for eternal life means you will stay gritty until the day you die. You will never lose your passion and your perseverance for the long-term goal to live forever. Unless you don't want to live forever, whatever the hell that looks like—but I do! And the way I plan to do that in the land of the living is with the Eternal Enterprise, which I am confident will not only live within my seeds, but with my seeds in the world at large. I am that bold to believe it, and I am damn sure that gritty. Stay gritty, baby.

Palumbo Principle 7: Execution Is Required at All Times

You will get nowhere fast if you fail to execute. The reason I have been so successful, and will continue to be successful, is because I am a LION. I am results-driven. I execute. What does execution look like? It looks like getting off your ass and getting to work. You can't just sit there, look at the plan you wrote, say, *"Hey, that looks great,"* and marvel at the way you were able to put some words on paper. That will never generate a dime. You must be disciplined and proactive. Execution often requires you to change your behavior. If you plan to achieve something you have never achieved before, you must do things you have never done. That takes a change in your behavior, and your mindset must be up to the challenge.

Another reason why people are often unable to execute is because they are trying to do too many things. You must narrow your focus. You need to stop multitasking. That only trains your brain to procrastinate. Multitasking is an illusion, as the brain only can work on one thing at a time. Your mental strength is everything when it comes to execution. To train your brain successfully, you need to learn to complete one project at a time. Treat your mind like a muscle. It takes time to build up muscle by going to the gym, lifting weights, and eating right. The same is true for your mind. Any weightlifter will tell you that you don't lift your arm weights and press legs at the same time. You do one exercise at a time. You do that with pure focus, deliberate practice, and repetition.

That same is true with execution. You get focused. You do. You build. You repeat. It is the new millennium, and *Entrepreneurship Empowered* requires you to be focused and to execute.

"Infuse your life with action. Don't wait for it to happen. Make it happen. Make your own future. Make your own hope. Make your own love."

—Bradley Whitford, actor

Palumbo Principle 6: We Don't Predict Our Future; We Create It

The sixth principle is one of my favorites because not only do I have the ability to be creative, I also have a very vast imagination. I have vision for lifetimes. I love the fact that, as an Empowered Entrepreneur, I will not predict my future, but rather I will create it, and that is indeed what I have been doing.

Prediction is unsure, but creation is a matter of fact. When you are creating, I want you to do more than just visualize. I want you to engage your senses. You see, when we bring the heart and the head together, there is nothing we cannot have or do. If you desire rain, don't just think about it and see it.... I need you to feel the rain on your face. I need you to smell the rain. I need you to walk around in your rain gear. This is how you activate a higher vibrational pull, and what you desire will come chasing after you. I have all kinds of vision boards—from poster boards to virtual ones that I keep on my phone. I am constantly making them. I put no time limit on the vision because, remember, though it may tarry, it is never late. It will be right on time. The vision is already ready. But it waits on you to be ready. It waits on divine alignment. Which is exactly what you want it to do.

This book and all the other books that I will write are on vision boards. The car I am currently driving was on a vision board. The money I am receiving from being a paid teacher is on a vision board. My wedding and marriage are on a vision board. And I promise you, the list goes on and on. I have one vision board right now manifesting at what seems to be the speed of light. So many things have all come to pass from this one vision board. What I can tell you is, I myself have become more aware of using my senses to feel my vision, as well as see it. This could well be the reason this one board is appearing ever so quickly. That and, well, I am ready. I am ready to truly receive what I desire.

Creating your future is true not only for personal life, but for business life as well. I was going to take over the U.S. with STFF, my core business. I stated before how I had marketing materials that were magnets the shape of the U.S., with my logo and my name and contact information on them. I also had other fact sheets that I would send out to my clients and to potential clients, which also had the U.S. on them. I was serious. I was coming for it. I didn't do too badly, truth be told. I captured 10% of the U.S. Imagine that. A welfare mom who became the CEO of her own company and went on to capture 10% of the U.S. I promise you, I did not predict that, nor could I have. But I sure had the vision to create it.

I will still take the other 90% of the U.S., and I plan to capture the globe as well. Both the U.S. and the globe are on several of my vision boards. I have seen myself traveling the world, speaking to seas upon seas of people, being the healer that I am. I know without a shadow of a doubt that I am the next top female speaker in the world and an award-winning author. This, too, is on a vision board. It is not only on a vision board, but I see it and feel it with my senses. My heart and my mind are in one accord. My vibrational level is elevated. I radiate at a very high frequency, which draws to me what I desire.

You can do the same. You must simply believe. You must remove the self-censor, which is in the center of your forehead. Do it now. Take your hand and place it on your forehead and grab it like you are going to pull your forehead off...but please don't do that, just play along. Grab your forehead and remove the self-censor. Just pull it off and throw that sucker away. Allow your creativity to take over. Believe in yourself and your vision. You don't need anyone else's approval to believe in yourself. And if you feel like you do need approval, you have just now been Professor Palumbo Approved! Boom! I want you to never stop building your vision boards, however you see fit to create them. I want you to always keep your head and heart in one accord when creating your future. It is the new millennium now. You are actually in the future because it is now.

Palumbo Principle 5: Sacrifice to Succeed

To be the crème de la crème of Empowered Entrepreneurs, you must understand that you will have to sacrifice in order to succeed. You will have to sacrifice sleep, food, relationships, parties, events, movies, news events, family time, and the like. This is what it will take for you to rise to the top. You will make the sacrifice, and if you have a family, they will need to be aware that not only are you going to make sacrifices, but they will, too. This can be the tricky part, especially for those of you who are married or have a significant other. If your spouse or partner is not on board with your vision and the direction you are going, you will need to figure out a way to get them on board. For your children, you will need to help them understand that the sacrifice will be well worth it in the end. That what you are doing is going to benefit them as well.

I am a firm believer in balance, so even though I have made many sacrifices, I have also made sure not to lose too much of myself and my time with my children. Everything else, however, I gave up. I don't watch TV. I don't even watch the news. (I do read—a lot.) I don't go out to parties. When others are partying it up on Friday or Saturday nights, I am grinding, or I am working out. I don't socialize, other than networking events to build my brand and business. I don't get caught up in family drama, and I have let go of several members of my family. I am a firm believer that *"family, friend, or foe—if they are toxic, you must let them go."* Unfortunately, too many of my family members are toxic, so I gave myself the gift of goodbye. I did this with friendships and with my foes. So many people are afraid to be alone, but being with abusive people is much worse than being alone. You are going to have to make the sacrifice to let them go and trust your vision. Trust where you are going and the purpose of your life.

There are many sayings out there along the lines of, *"You need to sacrifice like others will not in order to live like most never will."* This is so true. So many people will never even leave their backyard. Now, this isn't a bad thing if they are free and can take themselves to the ultra-limits while sitting in their backyard; for me, however, I could never just sit in my backyard. Nor would I. I can't sit still as it is, let alone in a yard. I need to be exposed to everything I possibly can. I desire to grow in culture and in character. I am planning for a hundred generations, if not more. In order to plan for that many generations, I must make the sacrifices. I cannot play around like others do; I must be working. The grind never stops.

I love holidays—not so much for the holiday itself, but for the fact that I get to grind. So, when I do desire to take a trip, I can do so without even blinking an eye. Which is exactly what I am about to do—my daughter and I are heading to Rome! I cannot tell you how many holidays I have worked and how many sleepless nights I have had grinding and building. But today I am reaping the fruit, and it only makes me hungrier. I am able to live now and still grind at the same time.

Emotional intelligence. Delayed gratification in action. I want you to think for a moment or two on what you know you need to sacrifice right now in order to succeed. Some of you need to really let go of some people and things in your life. It is not a sacrifice so much as a way to set yourself up, so you can level up. In the space provided, I want you to list all that comes to mind regarding letting go and sacrificing. I want you to start by asking yourself: *What do I really want from life? What am I willing to stop and start to get what I want for my life? Who's counting on me?* Answer those questions and write what comes to mind for sacrifice and letting go.

_____

_____
_____
_____
_____
_____
_____
_____
_____
_____
_____
_____
_____
_____
_____
_____
_____

Palumbo Principle 4: The Four Agreements

The Four Agreements is a book I highly recommend. The author is Don Miguel Ruiz. My uncle Michael gave me the book several years ago and encouraged me to read it. I ate it right up, and today I tell all my students about it. I have even considered adding it as a course requirement for one of the classes I teach, which deals with society and why we do what we do. Before I share with you what the Four Agreements are, I will share with you the even deeper message of the book: programming.

We have all been programmed since the moment of conception. Our programming makes us think a particular way. My mentor and dearest friend, Ron Hickey, says it best: *"If you don't have the courage to think critically for yourself, then someone will do the thinking for you, offering nothing substantive for your life. People have a way of pressuring you into complacency and maybe even pushing you into downright wretchedness. Before long, you rationalize your situation and learn to depend on others to do your every thinking."* Well, our parents really did all the thinking for us as children. They wired our brains, as well as the brains of others with whom we had contact. My grandfather, who abused me, certainly wired a lot of my brain. Today, I am successfully rewiring it.

You, too, have been wired, and your programming affects your everyday life. Then you connect with others who have been programmed, and you dance the night away, and even the day if you are so lucky, but many times you just end up dancing with demons. You eventually wake up and realize you have agreed to things you wouldn't truly agree to. The evolution of self and becoming more self-aware is critical in business and in life. I will tell you time and time again, because it is the truth, and I am here to help set you free. Once you begin to understand that you have been bound to agreements that are not yours, you begin—or should begin—to remove them and create new agreements. I call many of the agreements I had "generational curses," which I have broken. The new agreements I make are "generational blessings."

The Four Agreements are:

1. "***Be Impeccable with Your Word.*** *Speak with integrity. Say only what you mean. Avoid using words to speak against yourself or to gossip about others. Use the power of your Word in the direction of truth and love.*

2. ***Don't Take Anything Personally.*** *Nothing others do is because of you. What others say and do is a projection of their own reality, their own dream. When you are immune to the opinions and actions of others, you won't be the victim of needless suffering.*

3. ***Don't Make Assumptions.*** *Find the courage to ask questions and to express what you really want. Communicate with others as clearly as you can to avoid misunderstandings, sadness, and drama. With just this one agreement, you can completely transform your life.*

4. ***Always Do Your Best.*** *Your best is going to change from moment to moment; it will be different when you are healthy as opposed to sick. Under any circumstance, simply do your best, and you will avoid self-judgment, self-abuse, and regret.*"[27]

I love the fourth agreement the most. Because it is hard to live the other three agreements. However, I can tell you from personal experience—and with full confidence—that when you do live the other three, they hold great freedom. You become a spiritual warrior, and you ultimately become a master. A master of self. Ruiz has written several other books called the Mastery series, and I have read a few of them as well. Because one of my main issues has been self-hatred, I was drawn to one book in his series called *The Mastery of Love*, which is a collection of stories all geared to exposing and enlightening one on self-love. In the next principle, I am going to share with you a story from *The Mastery of Love*.

Palumbo Principle 3: The Story of the Star

The very last story I share with my students is the story of the star. As I stated prior, it comes from *The Mastery of Love.* It is absolutely one of my most favorite stories in the book.

The story is about a man who was very intelligent. He would travel around the world and speak to all kinds of people from many nations. His message: *Love does not exist.* That was his message. He would teach people the principle that love, as we know it, is not love. That real love did not exist at all. One day, the man was walking in a park, and along the trail he was walking, he came across a woman weeping on a park bench. He was taken by her and was concerned as to why she was weeping. He sat next to her ever so gently and inquired why she was weeping so.

The first thing she said was, "Love does not exist." He was taken aback because he spent the majority of his time convincing people that love does not exist, and here this woman was telling him what he told others. He inquired again, "How do you know that love does not exist?" She replied, "It could not. I loved my husband, or so I thought I did, and I thought he loved me too. I did everything he asked of me. I dressed the way he wanted. I cooked the way he liked. We had two beautiful children and I raised them the way he told me to. I did everything the way he instructed, and he left me after our youngest son left for college. Love does not exist. It is an illusion." The man replied, "You are correct, my dear. Love does not exist."

Now the man and the woman had this agreement that love did not exist, and they became friends. They would meet at the park regularly and share the day with each other. It didn't matter if they were having a good day or a bad day. They each accepted each other as they appeared from day to day. At that point, they were both operating in their authentic selves. There was no pressure to be anything other than the lily in the valley, as God designed them to be.

The days increased from meeting a few times a week to meeting almost daily. They truly enjoyed each other's company and began to wonder what they were really experiencing. Could it have been love they were experiencing, they questioned? So, they decided to become even closer because, of course, that is when it all changes, you know. They became a couple, and guess what? Nothing changed. They were their authentic selves. There was no pressure to be anything other than who they were.

So, they decided to take it even one step further. Because at this point, perhaps, love really did exist. But of course, marriage would surely kill it. So, they gave marriage a try. Yet again, they fell even more deeply in love. They had actually found love. They had found love in themselves to be who they were—their authentic selves. There was no pressure to be anything other than the lily in the valley, as God created them to be.

The man and the woman lived a very long life. When they were in their 90s, the man and woman were outside, and they were looking at the heavens. All of sudden, a star appeared in the sky and it headed right to the man. The most beautiful star you have ever seen was floating down ever so softly, and it landed in the man's hands. He was so taken by the star, but he loved the woman so much he wanted to give her the star. He turned toward her, and with the biggest smile on his face, he reached out his hand and placed the star in hers. The moment it landed in her hands she immediately dropped it and it shattered into a thousand pieces.

Why did it shatter, you ask? Because the star was never intended for her. The star was intended for him. She would have received her own star.

I need you to understand that you are a star holder. But the moment you place your star in anyone else's hands, it will shatter. What is so awesome about our God is that He takes our broken star, puts it back together again, and we have a stained-glass star that can still shine. But it must be in our own hands to shine. I know you want others to see how amazing your star is, and you just want them to touch it, but they cannot. If they do, they release the grip of their own star and will not shine. Far too often, I placed my star in others' hands and it shattered. Then I took my power back; I became emotionally intelligent, and I learned the power of delayed gratification. I made sacrifices, which included letting go of people and things that caused me more harm than good. I pulled away from agreements I never agreed to in the first place, and I began operating the best I could in the Four Agreements. I picked up my star and I began to shine. I became *EMPOWERED!*

When you are holding your star, you will attract other star holders. And what a beautiful community it will be. It will be love. Because love is the only thing that is real, everything else is an illusion. Love never dies, but it does transcend, as each of us will do one day. So LOVE, because that is what you are!

Palumbo Principle 2: You Have Rights to Your NO, and Your YES Is Undeniable

Did you know that you have rights to your "no"? Many people don't know this simple truth. For me, my "no" was taken at the age of three. My "no" was stolen. I didn't know how to say, *"No, don't touch me." "No, don't beat me." "No, don't treat me like that." "No, you can't have my money." "No, I can't take you there or here or everywhere."* And if you told me no, I would be absolutely crushed. *"No, I don't love you." "No, I can't help you." "No, you didn't get that job."* And so on.

But then I became *EMPOWERED* and took the rights to my life back, which included taking rights to my "no" back! I realized I let people walk all over me because I needed to feel like I belonged; that I was loved. But that was not love at all, and it only made me sicker. The side effects of abuse are nothing nice. My trauma side effects almost killed me. But God saw me through and He will see you through. I stopped being a people pleaser. I started saying "no" to others and "yes" to me. I became *EMPOWERED* and took my rights back. Being told "no" means nothing to me anymore because my YES is undeniable.

My ability to say "no" now has made me grow so much. I am much more balanced and healthier. Here's what is interesting: because I have started saying "no," I am able to serve at a much higher level than before. I have much more to offer in the right way, in a healthy way, and with complete purity of heart. I encourage you all to remember that you have rights to your "no," and your "yes" is undeniable. There is a time and a season for everything under the sun and in heaven. Your undeniable "yes" is found many times throughout your life and will certainly be found in heaven. You just need to allow that to remain at the forefront of your mind at all times. Your "yes" is far more powerful and purposeful than any "no" you will ever receive. As I stated before, I would be crushed to receive a "no," but my journey to becoming a professor is where I realized that my "yes" is undeniable. This powerful principle changed my life. I use this principle when I am creating my vision. I bring my senses in along with it and feel my undeniable "yes." I feel its power and purpose. I can see the "yes" appearing here and there. I know nothing is going to stop my "yes." Only I can stop it, and far too often, people do, because they don't know how to move past the "no" they just received.

As an Empowered Entrepreneur, you will be told "no" time and time again. These are the dice of life. But you are going to pick up those dice in your hands, shake them up, spit on them if you must, then throw them back to this world with all you have in you and say, "MY YES IS UNDENIABLE!" The power belongs to you.

Palumbo Principle 1: The Way Out Is Within

You are more powerful than you could even possibly imagine. *The way out is within.* No one is coming to save you. It is just that real. You can, however, save yourself. You were created in the image of the Most High God. Then He so graciously placed His lips on yours and blew breath into you. You are the image of God, and you have His breath in your lungs. What more do you really need?

For so many years, I wandered in the wilderness, searching and searching. One day, I came upon a large wooden door, and carved in the door in gigantic lettering was the word *VALIDATION*. *Oh boy,* I thought, *that is exactly what I need.* So, I knocked on the door, and all of a sudden, a guard appeared.

"What do you want?" the guard asked.

"Oh, I just want to come through this door."

"NO," the guard yelled back. "Go away."

I hung my head and away I walked. But I was determined to go through that door, so I thought to myself, *The guard will take an offering, I am sure. I will go get everything I can find. I will go dig up gold with my bare hands. I will search and collect, and I will search and collect some more, then I will take all that I have, all that I am, and give them to the guard.* I returned to the door and knocked. The guard appeared.

"What do you want?"

"I have everything I could gather. I have all the gold I could dig up, I have everything I possess, and I will give it all to you if you just let me through the door."

The guard took everything I had, then said, "NO, now go away. You cannot come through the door."

I then began to reflect: *Why am I the only one at the damn door. Where is everyone else?* The moment I had that epiphany, the guard stood up and pulled off a mask it was wearing to reveal to me who it really was. The damn guard was me.

We walk in the valley of validation and travel in the forest of falsehood, only to finally realize that the door we so desperately want to walk through, we are guarding ourselves. *The way out is within.* You must pull the mask off, take a cold, hard look at yourself, and decide that you will no longer seek approval from those who will turn to dust just like you. We all die, my friends. Not one of us gets to stay, nor do I believe we would really want to, truth be told. But I am a firm believer we can build something that will outlast time. This is why I work so hard. This is why I am determined to share with the world what I know and the keys I have used to be free.

I need you to no longer underestimate your willpower. I need you to turn your "I wish" into "I will." Stop making wishes and blowing hot air everywhere. Change your wish to "I will" and then execute. Many of you are still waiting for a wish to come true when all you have to do is go make it happen. I am a firm believer that anything is possible, and wishes do come true. But you must be action-oriented. The power of will is extremely important to understand and activate at the highest vibrational frequency. How did God create the world? His WILL. Will is all the power that exists. We don't use enough of it. We become lazy and say a wish or two instead of working our God-given power to manifest the miracles in our life. Once you recognize that your willpower is your God-given power, it will increase and show you more than you could ever begin to wish for.

"The way out is within."

—Natasha M Palumbo, author and speaker

I now leave you with one final activity. Then I will send you on your way, and my confidence is that you leave much differently than when you came. I am sending you out the door EMPOWERED! The dictionary defines empowered as "*made (someone) stronger and more confident, **especially in controlling their life and claiming their rights.***" In the space provided, you are going to write your personal empowerment statement. You will also set three goals: a three-month, six-month, and one-year goal. I have provided my empowerment statement and goals as examples.

For your empowerment statement, I want you to tell me what area in your life you would like to be more *EMPOWERED*. What steps will you take to become more *EMPOWERED*? Then move into goal setting. Be realistic, but let it be a bit of a challenge. Remember, *the way out is within*, and freedom comes in pieces.

Thank you for being with me. It has been my honor.
Be *EMPOWERED.*

Empowered Statement—My Example:

I am a people-pleaser, and many times have become so hurt by family, friends, and people in general. What I am learning is that it is very unhealthy to be a people-pleaser. It can actually make you sick and has many times made me sick. The side effects of abuse are nothing nice. Being a people-pleaser is one of my side effects. But I am healing and will continue to heal and be free. I have decided to be *EMPOWERED* and no longer subject myself to people-pleasing. I will choose to say "no" and have no remorse. I will say "YES" to me. I am confident in myself and the purpose of my life. I know that I am not able to please everyone, nor will I inspire everyone, but I have had visions where I have seen seas upon seas of people who will be inspired by my life story. I will be used to give hope to so many that feel hopeless. I will be used to help heal and set others free. This pleases me.

Goals:

    3-month: Run a 10K

    6-month: Take a vacation

    1-year: Lose 25 pounds

Now, it is your turn....

_____

_____

_____

_____

_____

_____

_____

_____

_____

_____

_____
_____
_____
_____
_____
_____
_____
_____
_____
_____
_____
_____
_____
_____
_____
_____
_____
_____
_____
_____
_____
_____
_____
_____
_____
_____

ENTREPRENEURSHIP
EMPOWERED

A New Millennium Business Guide from Start Up to Succession

Answer Key

Kid Tested. Mother Approved.
Life's Good
Trusted Everywhere
Maybe She's Born With It
We Try Harder
Keep Walking
Gather 'Round the Good Stuff
Makes Mouths Happy
Something Special in the Air
It's Not Just a Job, It's an Adventure!

Kix Cereal — The famous low sugar, round cereal!
LG Electronics — LG manufactures high quality flat panel televisions.
Duracell Batteries — Called "The Coppertop"
Maybelline — Maybelline was started in 1915!
Avis — Avis is headquartered in Parsippany, New Jersey.
Johnnie Walker — Johnnie Walker Scotch Whiskey is produced in Scotland.
Pizza Hut — Pizza Hut is owned by the same company that owns Taco Bell.
Twizzlers — Twizzlers flavors include chocolate, strawberry and watermelon.
American Airlines — American Airlines is headquartered in Ft. Worth, Texas.
Navy — The Department of the Navy is a division of the Department of Defense.

References and Resources

The following resources were used in writing this book and are duly noted in the text:

[1] Neck, Heidi M., Neck, Christopher P., and Murray, Emma L. (2016.) *Entrepreneurship: The Practice and Mindset.* SAGE Publications.

[2] "Frequently Asked Questions About Small Business." (2019.) U.S. Small Business Administration. Accessed January 12, 2020.
https://cdn.advocacy.sba.gov/wp-content/uploads/2019/09/23172241/Frequently-Asked-Questions-Small-Business-20191.pdf.

[3] Swanbrow, Diane. "Empathy: College Students Don't Have as Much as They Used To." (2010.) University of Michigan News. Accessed January 12, 2020.
https://news.umich.edu/empathy-college-students-don-t-have-as-much-as-they-used-to/.

[4] Daniel, C. "The 4 Animals Assessment." (n.d.). The 4 Animals Experience. Accessed December 20, 2019.
https://4animalsassessment.com/page-29740388.

[5] Kendall Ficklin's Grindation website:
www.grindation.com.

[6] "Albert Mehrabian Communication Studies." (n.d.) Institute of Judicial Studies. Accessed January 12, 2020.
http://www.iojt-dc2013.org/~/media/Microsites/Files/IOJT/11042013-Albert-Mehrabian-Communication-Studies.ashx.

[7] Giang, Vivian. "7 Email Etiquette Rules Every Professional Should Know." (2014.) Accessed January 12, 2020. https://www.careerbuilder.com/advice/seven-email-etiquette-rules-every-professional-should-know.

[8] O'Hara, Carolyn. "How to Improve Your Business Writing." (2014.) *Harvard Business Review*. Accessed January 12, 2020. https://hbr.org/2014/11/how-to-improve-your-business-writing.

[9] National Association of Colleges and Employers website: https://www.naceweb.org/.

[10] "The Future of Jobs and Skills." (2016.) World Economic Forum. Accessed January 13, 2020. http://reports.weforum.org/future-of-jobs-2016/chapter-1-the-future-of-jobs-and-skills/#view/fn-1.

[11] 17hats website: https://www.17hats.com/.

[12] Rouse, Margaret, Lutkevich, Ben, and Bigelow, Stephen J. "What Is a Private Cloud and What Are Its Advantages?" (n.d.) TechTarget. Accessed January 13, 2020. https://searchcloudcomputing.techtarget.com/definition/private-cloud.

[13] Hwong, Connie. "How Consumers Spend Their Time Online." (2018.) Verto Analytics. Accessed January 13, 2020. https://vertoanalytics.com/how-consumers-spend-time-online/.

[14] GoDaddy website: https://www.godaddy.com/.

[15] Small Business Administration (SBA) website: https://www.sba.gov.

[16] Fairbrothers, Gregg and Gorla, Catalina. "What Exactly Is Social Entrepreneurship?" (2012.) Forbes. Accessed January 13, 2020.

https://www.forbes.com/sites/greggfairbrothers/2012/05/28/what-exactly-is-social-entrepreneurship/#50e9ee393da0.

[17] Berger, Jonah. (2016.) *Contagious: Why Things Catch On.* Published by Simon & Schuster. New York: New York.

[18] Active Marketing website:

https://www.activemarketing.com/our-work/.

[19] Ou, Amy Y., Waldman, David A., and Peterson, Suzanne J. "Do Humble CEOs Matter?" (2015.) *Journal of Management.* Accessed January 13, 2020.

https://createvalue.org/wp-content/uploads/Do-Humble-CEOs-Matter.pdf.

[20] Glazer, Robert. "How Training Like a Pilot Will Set You Up for Success." (2018.) Forbes. Accessed January 13, 2020.

https://www.forbes.com/sites/robertglazer/2018/07/13/how-training-like-a-pilot-will-set-you-up-for-success-in-crisis-management/#62059d1f7dde.

[21] "What is Transformational Leadership? How New Ideas Produce Impressive Results." (2014.) STU online. Accessed January 13, 2020.

https://online.stu.edu/articles/education/what-is-transformational-leadership.aspx.

[22] "What Are Business Ethics?" (n.d.) Corporate Finance Institute. Accessed January 13, 2020.

https://corporatefinanceinstitute.com/resources/knowledge/other/business-ethics/.

[23] IRS website:

https://www.irs.gov./.

[24] Workable website: https://www.workable.com/.

[25] New World of Work website: https://newworldofwork.org/.

[26] Nolo website: https://www.nolo.com/.

[27] Ruiz, Don Miguel. (1997.) *The Four Agreements: A Practical Guide to Personal Freedom*. Amber-Allen Publishing, Inc. San Rafael, California.

About the Author

Ms. Palumbo is a business professional with more than 20 years of experience—17 as an entrepreneur. She is a creative leader with in-depth knowledge and expertise applying strategic business management, development of small business initiatives, and progressive leadership. Ms. Palumbo is an effective communicator with an innate ability to engage and hold the attention of those she trains and teaches. She owns several businesses, and she successfully grew her core business into multiple states. She is a social entrepreneur and has been serving the homeless community for more than 15 years. In addition to being an Empowered Entrepreneur, Ms. Palumbo is a Business Adjunct professor for several colleges in the greater Sacramento region.

Natasha M Palumbo, MBA
Author, Coach, Consultant and Speaker
Entrepreneur – Educator – Empowered

Instagram and LinkedIn: Natasha M Palumbo

natasha@entrepreneurshipempowered.com